ENCOUNTERING
CHRIST THE SERVANT

ENCOUNTERING
CHRIST
THE SERVANT

A SPIRITUALITY OF THE DIACONATE

DEACON DOMINIC CERRATO, PH.D.
FOREWORD BY SCOTT HAHN

Our Sunday Visitor
Huntington, Indiana

Nihil Obstat
Msgr. Michael Heintz, Ph.D.
Censor Librorum

Imprimatur
✠ Kevin C. Rhoades
Bishop of Fort Wayne-South Bend
May 20, 2020

The *Nihil Obstat* and *Imprimatur* are official declarations that a book is free from doctrinal or moral error. It is not implied that those who have granted the *Nihil Obstat* and *Imprimatur* agree with the contents, opinions, or statements expressed.

The author would like to acknowledge gratefully the assistance of Laurie Malashanko and Anisha Verma-Virgen.

Our Sunday Visitor Publishing Division
Our Sunday Visitor, Inc.
200 Noll Plaza
Huntington, IN 46750
www.osv.com
1-800-348-2440
ISBN: 978-1-68192-436-6 (Inventory No. T2323)
RELIGION—Christianity—Catholic.
RELIGION—Christian Ministry—Pastoral Resources.
RELIGION—Clergy.

eISBN: 978-1-68192-437-3
LCCN: 2020938798

Cover and interior design: Amanda Falk
Cover art: Jesus Christ washes the feet of St. Peter while the other apostles watch in astonishment at the Last Supper. Artwork by F. Brown/Restored Traditions
Interior art: Renata Sedmakova / Shutterstock.com, AdobeStock

PRINTED IN THE UNITED STATES OF AMERICA

*To my loving wife, Judith,
and our children — Maria,
Theresa, Anthony,
Dominic, Christina, Michael,
Gabriella, Catherine, Daniel,
and Joseph — all of
whom have taught me
what it means to be a good
and faithful servant.*

Contents

Foreword *by Dr. Scott Hahn*   9

Introduction   13
    The Search for Intimacy   13
    Beginning the Journey   16
    Extending Diaconal Spirituality to the Laity   21

Chapter One: The Primacy of the Interior Life   25
    The Interior Life as a Place of Encounter   27
    The Distinctiveness of Diaconal Spirituality   30
    The Importance of Empathy   33
    Struggle in the Spiritual Life   36
    The Unholy Trinity and Sloth   37
    Grace Is the Remedy   41
    Surrender Is Abandonment   43
    Struggle as a Way of Perfection   45

Chapter Two: The Necessity of Abandonment   53
    Awareness of the Ever-Present God   59
    God's Hidden Operations   62
    The Sacrament of the Present Moment   69

Chapter Three: The Servant Mysteries   75
    A Beauty That Wounds   76
    Keeping Open the Wounds   83
    Internalizing the Servant Mysteries   94
    Applying the Sacrament of the Present Moment   97

Chapter Four: Living the Servant Mysteries 103

Revealing the Origins of the Diaconate 105
Reconciling Acts 6 with the Establishment 111
Relationship, Identity, and Mission 112
Putting It All Together 120
Prayer of Abandonment and Little Examen 124

Conclusion 129
Appendix 131

Foreword

By Dr. Scott Hahn

There is something paradoxical in the way we experience the diaconate today. For Catholics of a certain age, it is a modern innovation. It was proposed by the Second Vatican Council in 1964 and launched by Pope Paul VI in 1967. Dioceses worldwide began forming men for the diaconate immediately, and initial interest ran especially high in the United States. So Catholics watched the diaconate go from zero to ninety in what seemed like seconds.

And it is indeed a modern reality — but it is *not* an innovation. In fact, the diaconate is modern because it is ancient.

The Fathers of the early Church found the deepest roots of the diaconate not in the New Testament, but in the Old. The structure of the Catholic Church — as described by Ignatius of Antioch in A.D. 107 — is foreshadowed in the worship of Israel's tabernacle and Temple. The holy place was attended by a high priest, assisted by other priests who made sacrificial offerings; and these assisting priests were attended in turn by Levites who were given certain fundamental tasks of holy service. The men in this third category might sing the psalms of David, or play musical instruments, or even work in the construction crews that built the Temple (there was a tradition that the stones and mortar should be set in place only by consecrated men).

A similar tripartite division of the clergy appears immediately with the emergence of the Christian Church. The Acts of the Apostles and the epistles of Saint Paul speak of bishops (see, for example, 1 Tm 3:1), presbyters (1 Pt 5:1), and deacons (1 Tm 3:8–13). The roles seem to have been somewhat fluid in that first generation, and there would be clarification and development through the pre-Nicene era. But certainly by the time of the First Council of Nicaea the identity of each order of clergy was settled and well defined.

Throughout its first few centuries, deacons enjoyed great prominence in the Church. Two of the most beloved figures of Christian antiquity are Lawrence of Rome and Ephrem of Syria, both permanent deacons. The vast majority of the popes of the early Church were chosen *not* from the ranks of the presbyters but from the ranks of the deacons. Jerome, in the fifth century, wryly observed that when a bishop wanted to demote a deacon, he simply ordained him a priest.

So it was. But as the Western Church became the establishment, the office of deacon diminished almost to a vanishing point. The diaconate became almost exclusively a way station on the way to priesthood. However, the memory remained, and now and then the office was filled in a permanent way by an extraordinary saint. I need mention no other than Francis of Assisi.

We see then how the diaconate is ancient — but in what

sense is it modern? As I said at the start, it is modern because it is ancient.

Three streams of thought — three intellectual currents — flowed into the Second Vatican Council: the biblical movement, the liturgical movement, and the patristic movement. All three had bubbled to the surface of Catholic scholarship in the nineteenth century and overflowed their banks in the first half of the twentieth. All three were movements of retrieval. Taken together, they represented a phenomenon known by the French word *ressourcement*. They were a "return to the sources" of Christian tradition.

In those sources, we (in the Western Church) rediscovered the permanent diaconate, and we restored it for the renewal of Christian life.

Just a week ago, I watched as my son was ordained to the order of deacons, and I experienced the richness of the rite. I witnessed also the affection that seems consubstantial with the office. The liturgy speaks of service and fraternity, and both themes play out in the postures, gestures, and even vestments of those who are celebrating. The signs are rich and profound — and real. When the deacons of the diocese embraced their new brother, my eyes underwent a sudden surge from those three subterranean currents: biblical, liturgical, and patristic.

Or maybe I was moved to tears.

Deacons are united in their spirit of service. It's something they can never put aside. They're united not only locally but universally — and not only within the Church militant, but with the Church triumphant. The deacons who serve my parish today are not descendants of Lawrence and Ephrem; they are their contemporaries and brothers.

I am deeply grateful to my colleague Deacon Dominic Cerrato for setting himself the task of describing the beautiful spirit that these men share across the centuries. His work — expressed in this book and in his churchmanship — is an important contribution to the retrieval and renewal still happening in the Church. We are all beneficiaries.

Introduction

My little children, your hearts are small, but prayer stretches them and makes them capable of loving God. Through prayer we receive a foretaste of heaven and something of paradise comes down upon us. Prayer never leaves us without sweetness. It's honey that flows into the souls and makes all things sweet. When we pray properly, sorrows disappear like snow before the sun.
Saint John Vianney, *Catechetical Instructions*, Office of Readings, August 4

THE SEARCH FOR INTIMACY

This year, as I celebrate my silver jubilee, I'm deeply grateful for the gift of Christ the Servant in my diaconate, in my marriage, in my fatherhood, and indeed in the whole of my life. This appreciation, interestingly enough, is made more profound by my recognition that I often struggle with the interior life. Sure, I pray my breviary, receive spiritual direction, frequent the Sacrament of Reconciliation, partake in the Eucharist regularly, and dutifully perform all the obligations associated with my vocation. Still, I'm not, at my core, a contemplative man, at least not in the sense that many of the saints and mystics were. It's not easy for me to suffer the presence of Christ at adoration, to dedicate time to Him in *lectio*, to meditate upon Him quietly for any significant period.

Strange as it may seem, my lack of a natural affinity for prayer and the interior struggles associated with this lack have brought me to an ever-increasing realization that what is difficult in the spiritual life is often necessary. This isn't to say that I haven't made some slow progress over the years, but rather that the progress I've made, with God's grace, has yet to bring me to the intimacy I so desire. In this struggle, I suspect I'm not alone.

This work represents a spiritual journey for me. Over the past several years, I have developed a theology of the diaconate based on the thought of Pope Saint John Paul II.[1] In this pursuit, I have been consoled by a Dominican approach to interiority that integrates the intellectual and spiritual aspects of life and has enabled me to experience theology as an encounter with the living God. One of Saint Dominic de Guzmán's most significant contributions to the Catholic spiritual tradition is the belief that theological endeavor, particularly as it pertains to the Word of God, isn't simply an aid to prayer but an act of worship itself — an act that sanctifies.

Nowhere is this Dominican integration of the spiritual and intellectual life more beautifully illustrated than in an account of the thirteenth-century Dominican priest Saint Thomas Aquinas. Having written volumes on a wide range of theological and philosophical issues, Saint Thomas was and is a towering figure

---

[1] Dominic Cerrato, *In the Person of Christ the Servant: A Theology of the Diaconate Based on the Personalist Approach of Pope John Paul II* (Bloomingdale, OH: St. Ephraem Press, 2014).

in Catholic intellectual circles. Yet his intellect was exceeded by his sanctity, as witnessed by the great hymns he wrote for the feast of Corpus Christi, hymns we still sing today. One morning toward the end of his life, Thomas was in the priory chapel, kneeling before the crucifix absorbed in prayer, as was his usual practice. Unknown to him, Brother Dominic of Caserta, a sacristan, was close by and witnessed an extraordinary scene. Breaking the silence, a great voice boomed from the crucifix, saying in Latin, "You've written well of me Thomas. What will you have as your reward?" Saint Thomas answered, *"Non nisi te Domine. Non nisi te"* ("Nothing but you, Lord. Nothing but you"). Thomas understood well that the intellectual life is at the service of the spiritual life. His pursuit of truth, though noble in itself, was ultimately a pursuit of the Truth, Jesus Christ (see Jn 14:6). In this respect, the only response Thomas could utter, the only response that made sense, was *"Non nisi te Domine."* He knew in the core of his being that no reward is greater than intimate communion with God himself.

Despite my struggles with the interior life, in the doing of theology, especially in plumbing the sources of Revelation, I have found myself wrapped in the Divine Presence. For me theology is, as Saint Anselm of Canterbury so succinctly put it, "faith seeking understanding." From this perspective, I can see, like Aquinas, that the teachings I study aren't cold, dispassionate doctrines, distinct and separate from my spiritual life, but truths that mediate the Truth. Theology, for me, isn't the search for something but the discovery of Someone. It is about falling in love with God. In this sense, my interior life has moved beyond a mere intellectual pursuit. Nonetheless, I have slowly become more aware that what has been lacking in me as a deacon is a deeper, more intimate communion with Christ the Servant. Sure, I know Him theologically in the Scriptures and Tradition. I have experienced Him in worship through the sacraments. I have encountered Him pastorally in ministry. However, none of these on its own has brought the deep intimacy I so desire.

This yearning to draw closer to Christ the Servant has been and continues to be quite palpable. After much prayer, it has struck me that my spirituality, with its integration of the intellectual life, isn't an obstacle in pursuing this greater intimacy but the very path to it. I have realized that I can't love what I don't first understand. To describe what I mean in more figurative language, the head and the heart don't work in isolation, but rather the head works with the heart, each contributing something unique. In this integration, God doesn't disappoint. On the contrary, rich insights have emerged, particularly regarding the interior life related to my diaconate. I have found myself taken up, often wrapped in Christ's presence, and in this place have developed a greater desire for adoration, a yearning for more *lectio*, and the longing to just be with Him. I still have a considerable way to go, but the working out of this book has moved me to be more sensitive to the Divine Presence, especially the presence of Christ the Servant as He is revealed in the Servant Mysteries. Though greater detail will follow, it is sufficient at this time to define the Servant Mysteries as the revelation of Christ the Servant as made known in the present moment.

BEGINNING THE JOURNEY

Always remember this: life is a journey. It is a path, a journey to meet Jesus. At the end, and forever. ... It is for the Christian to continually encounter Jesus, to watch him, to let himself be watched over by Jesus, because Jesus watches us with love. ... To encounter Jesus also means allowing oneself to be gazed upon by him.
Pope Francis, Pastoral Visit to the Roman Parish of Saint Cyril of Alexandria, December 1, 2013

All spiritual journeys begin with a call, an interior movement of the heart that beckons us to travel from where we are to where we need to be. The Church speaks of the Christian life in terms of a "call" or "vocation," derived from the Latin term *vocatio*. Classically, vocations are divided into specific categories such as priestly, diaconal, married, consecrated, and lay. While helpful, such categorical distinctions, left unqualified, can hide more than they reveal. This is because we can fixate upon them such that we fail to see that they are means to a greater end. Pope Saint John Paul II writes:

> God is love and in himself He lives a mystery of personal loving communion. Creating the human race in His own image and continually keeping it in being, God inscribed in the humanity of man and woman the vocation, and thus the capacity and responsibility, of love and communion. Love is therefore the fundamental and innate vocation of every human being.[2]

Love of God and love of neighbor (see Mk 12:30–31) constitute the universal vocation to which all human beings are called. The particular vocations (such as the priestly, diaconal, married, consecrated, and lay vocations) are ordered to this universal vocation. Put another way, the particular vocations are the journey through which we experience the universal vocation — that is, intimate communion with God. Viewing a particular vocation as an end in itself is like looking at a pointing finger instead of looking at the direction in which the finger points. It fails to recognize that all of these vocations are contextualized in their final end: love of God and love of neighbor. Understood this way, our vocations are not so much *to* something as *through* something to Someone, Christ Jesus. This approach, rather than stressing the

---

[2] *Familiaris Consortio*, 11.

difference between calls, instead emphasizes what is common. In doing so, it reveals both what is most essential and the end to which all human life is ordered. The source of the deacon's particular vocation, the very foundation of his life and ministry, is intimate communion with Christ the Servant. This universal vocation originates from and deepens within the interior life, that inner place where the deacon is alone with himself. It's here, through prayer and meditation, that he truly discovers God on a personal level and, at the same time, discovers himself in a more profound way.

For Catholics serious about their faith, the interior life is shaped by a love of Jesus Christ as He is revealed through His Church. This means that their piety, core values, and subsequent actions should conform to this belief. In a similar way, for a Catholic deacon serious about his diaconate, the interior life is shaped both by his Catholic faith and by how that faith is enriched and specified by his vocation to bear witness to Christ the Servant. Consequently, his piety, core values, and subsequent actions should conform to this belief.

The doorway to the interior life is through the deacon's own spirituality. By spirituality, I mean a life lived in the Holy Spirit, given to us by the Father through His Son. Spirituality is a participation in the life of the Triune God. More discovered from within than appropriated from without, the spirituality of a deacon, in a broad sense, can take many forms — Benedictine, Franciscan, Dominican, Ignatian, and Carmelite, to name a few. Beyond merely offering access to the interior life, these spiritualities also provide a means to nourish it. Just as the soul infuses the body with life, so too does a deacon's spirituality imbue his life with the love of God.

While most would readily acknowledge this fundamental truth, many diaconal publications and formation programs tend to relegate spirituality to one distinct and separate element among the four elements of diaconal formation (which also include the intellectual, pastoral, and human dimensions). This approach is seriously flawed as it fragments formation and, in the process, the one being formed. It fails to see formation as an integrative, lifelong endeavor in which the candidate becomes more fully who he is through "one sole organic journey."[1] These dimensions must be fused together, and that fusion is accomplished by the spiritual life. It's the spiritual dimension that enables the intellect to grasp the truth more fully, the pastoral to serve the Church more effectively, and the human to relate to others more authentically. Together, in an organic fashion, the spiritual, intellectual, pastoral, and human dimensions represent a course of integration that capacitates a man for sacred ecclesial service, continuing to perfect his ministry and, in the process, his very self.

The purpose of this book is to help deacons grow in greater intimacy with Christ the Servant. Beginning with the primacy of the interior life, it explores the nature of the deacon's interiority, focusing on that which makes diaconal spirituality truly diaconal. Here, the importance of empathy is examined, along with the struggles encountered in the spiritual life. This is followed by a consideration of abandonment to divine providence as an essential aspect of interiority, with special emphasis on the deacon's need to surrender to Christ the Servant. This surrender reveals, in the sacrament of the present moment, the Servant Mysteries — that is, Christ the Servant as He is manifested in the life and ministry of the deacon. Finally, this work grounds a life lived in the Servant Mysteries in a new look at the origins of the diaconate and how this pertains to a deacon's relationship to, identity in, and mission with Christ the Servant.

In all of this, great emphasis is placed on situating our con-

---

[1] United States Conference of Catholic Bishops, *National Directory for the Formation, Ministry, and Life of Permanent Deacons in the United States* (Washington, DC: USCCB Publishing, 2005), 104.

sideration of the diaconate within the broader Catholic spiritual and mystical traditions and on providing a sense of continuity with those same traditions. To that end, quotes from saints and mystics are sprinkled throughout, adding a depth and dimension to what is discussed. While the restored diaconate is relatively new, the tradition from which it emerges is ancient and rich. This tradition, along with recent theological developments, provides the necessary framework on which to build an authentically Catholic diaconal spirituality.

In writing this book and presenting my thoughts, I don't wish to imply that I'm some sort of spiritual master or even an authority on mystical and spiritual theology. I come as one poor beggar showing other poor beggars where the food is. This work merely represents my own ponderings as they've been shaped by my own particular theological and spiritual formation within the Catholic tradition. I'm convinced that what I've stumbled upon is meant not just for me but for any and all who might benefit from it. In this, I humbly lay at your feet, my dear brother deacons, whatever worth you find in this book so that, together and in union with Him, we may bear witness to Christ the Servant, fulfilling our vocations and contributing to the mission of the Church.

One final note before beginning: Do not let the brevity of this book fool you. It's packed with insights to be carefully unpacked in the heart of the reader. If you read this book in a cursory way, it will reveal little and later sit on the shelf collecting dust. Instead, I invite you to read this text in a deeply prayerful and contemplative state. Take it in small bits, as in the practice of *lectio divina*: As you read, ask Our Lord to reveal in your heart what you need to know and how what He reveals should impact the whole of your life. Look for yourself among the pages, and discover in your reflection what you are and what you're called to be. Patiently waiting for you within these very pages is none other than Christ the Servant. Go and meet Him with great joy.

EXTENDING DIACONAL SPIRITUALITY TO THE LAITY

As any quick online search will reveal, there is a wide variety of books on Catholic spirituality. From classics such as Saint Augustine's *Confessions* to more contemporary works such as Saint Josemaría Escrivá's *The Way of the Cross*, the Catholic spiritual tradition is replete with a dazzling array of books. Even so, there are few written especially for deacons and even fewer that take up diaconal spirituality. This book is meant to address that lack and, in the process, explore that which is particular to the diaconate.

As I worked through these chapters and shared some of my insights with family and friends, they encouraged me to write a second, similar book directed to the laity. After further prayer and reflection, it struck me that while distinctively diaconal, much of the content of this book would appeal to the "deacon" in every baptized person. This is precisely why the laity with whom I shared my early drafts could identify with the substance of my work and, more to the point, see its relevance in their own spiritual lives. As a result, after the publication of this book, I will again take up my pen and write another, this time directed to a lay spirituality rooted in intimate communion with Christ the Servant.

To better appreciate why the laity can benefit from what can be described as a *servant spirituality*, we need to contextualize it within the universal call to discipleship. All active Christians are, by definition, followers of Christ. In His mission of salvation, Jesus identified himself as a servant (see Mt 20:28; Mk 10:45). In this respect, all Christians, as disciples, are called to serve as Christ served, evangelizing others and, at the same time, cooperating in their own personal sanctification. Each vocation — be it priestly, diaconal, consecrated, married, or lay — serves and contributes to the mission of the Church in a particular way, with the combination of the vocations revealing Jesus Christ most fully. That said, it would be a mistake to see these vocations in complete isolation. To be sure, they are each distinct, but each interacts with the others in varying degrees and, in doing so, enriches the others. For example, only certain men are called to the priesthood, yet the Church points out that all vocations possess a priestly quality, an element of sacrifice. According to the *Catechism of the Catholic Church*:

> Christ, high priest and unique mediator, has made of the Church "a kingdom, priests for his God and Father." The whole community of believers is, as such, priestly. The faithful exercise their baptismal priesthood through their participation, each according to his own vocation, in Christ's mission as priest, prophet, and king. Through the sacraments of Baptism and Confirmation the faithful are "consecrated to be ... a holy priesthood." (1546)

What is true of the priesthood is equally true of the diaconate. Just as the priesthood bears witness to Christ the Priest, so too does the diaconate bear witness to Christ the Servant. Indeed, just as the ordained priesthood inspires and enriches the priesthood of the laity, so too does the ordained diaconate inspire and enrich the servanthood of that same laity. Practically speaking, this means that those called to the vocation of marriage are to serve their spouses and children with the quality of service revealed by Christ Jesus. To put it another way, each vocation interacts with the others, deepening and perfecting the others such that, together, they more effectively advance God's plan of salvation. In the context of the diaconate, this complementarity means that those with vocations other than the diaconate can benefit from knowing more about Christ the Servant, learning from Him what it means to be a true servant as they live out their own particular vocations.

This understanding reveals the universality of the diaconate expressed, in this case, through a *servant spirituality*. In its most basic sense, the term "servant" is translated from the Greek word *diakonos*, from which we get the English word "deacon." Christians share in Christ's own mission and thus they share in His own servanthood, His own diaconate. Just as Christ's servanthood was, and is, an essential aspect of His identity and mission, so too is it an essential part, albeit in different ways, of the identity and mission of all who call themselves Christians. If this identification of the laity with Christ the Servant seems somewhat vague, perhaps an analogy would be helpful. As noted above, the *Catechism* observes that there are two participations in the one priesthood of Christ, teaching that "Christ, high priest and unique mediator, has made of the Church, 'a kingdom, priests for his God and Father.' The whole community of believers is, as such, priestly". It goes on to say:

> The ministerial or hierarchical priesthood of bishops and priests, and the common priesthood of all the faithful participate, "each in its own proper way, in the one priesthood of Christ." While being "ordered one to another," they differ essentially. ... While the common priesthood of the faithful is exercised by the unfolding of baptismal grace ... the ministerial priesthood is at the service of the common priesthood. It is directed at the unfolding of the baptismal grace of all Christians. (1547)

If this is true of the priesthood, and it is, then might it also be true of the diaconate? Could there be two participations in the one diaconate of Christ?

Because the laity share, by virtue of their Baptism, in the

one diaconate of Christ, this common diaconate means that lay Catholics would naturally find an affinity with the insights in this book. They would not only identify with the spiritual principles common to all Christians, but likewise see the importance of the Servant Mysteries of Christ in the Gospels, along with their unique contribution to God's plan of salvation. It is hoped that this book will not only provide deacons with ongoing spiritual formation for themselves, but that it will also equip them to help lay Catholics grow in greater intimacy with Christ the Servant. This effort, with grace, will enable them to become better husbands and wives, fathers and mothers, sons and daughters, friends and neighbors.

It is my heartfelt desire that the insights my fellow deacons gain from this work will inspire them to form a new diaconal ministry, in which deacons lead parish study groups, drawing the laity into a greater appreciation of their own role of service within the Church. In this respect, the deacon, who is called to bear witness to Christ the Servant, can now do so by teaching others to extend that same witness into their own vocation. In this way he broadens his ministry to people and places beyond his normal reach and influence, fulfilling his ministry in a unique and highly effective manner. This extended diaconal ministry is only possible, only effective, if the deacon enters into the spirituality found in this book and makes it his own.

Chapter One
The Primacy of the Interior Life

What more do you want, O soul! And what else do you search for outside, when within yourself you possess your riches, delights, satisfactions, fullness, and kingdom — your Beloved whom you desire and seek? Be joyful and gladdened in your interior recollection with Him, for you have Him so close to you. Desire Him there, adore Him there.
Saint John of the Cross, *Spiritual Canticle*

Ours is not so much an outward search for God but a desire to discover Him from within. The God who created us, who loved us into being, who died for us while we were still sinners, is already present in our interior lives, waiting patiently to be encountered and reencountered. While He is certainly present in the world around us — in the people we meet, in the situations we confront — that outward presence goes largely unnoticed and unappreciated without an inward recognition. Our ability to see Christ in those we serve begins with an interior life attuned to His Divine Presence.

It's only in the interior life that the deacon comes to know and love Christ the Servant, to whom he was configured on the day of his ordination. As expressed succinctly in the first lesson of the *Baltimore Catechism*, knowing and loving God are absolute preconditions for serving Him. This is because we simply can't love whom we don't know. But knowing God isn't merely understanding Him — to the extent possible — on an intellectual level through the study of faith, though this is essential. Without exposure to and immersion in such sources as the Scriptures, Tradition, and the Magisterium, we couldn't speak the name of Christ, much less know Him. However, to truly know Him is to move in, through, and beyond this study (which is a lifetime endeavor) to a deep, interpersonal relationship, sharing in His very life. This is only possible through the cultivation of an interior life.

Relationships, if they are healthy, are always mutual in that they admit of a kind of reciprocity that ought to grow in intimacy and tenderness over time. In deepening our relationship with God through perfection in the spiritual life, we come, ever so slowly at first, to see ourselves as God sees us, albeit in a limited way. This wondrous self-revelation enables us to begin to appreciate our real self-worth. We are, as Jesus demonstrated so beautifully on the Cross, worth dying for. Entering into this truth helps us to see that everything we have, every event we experience, whether triumph or tragedy, is a gift from God.

THE INTERIOR LIFE AS A PLACE OF ENCOUNTER

When we prayerfully reflect on these gifts, when we meditate upon their implications, we discover in and through them the Giver — we encounter none other than God himself. These gifts are, in many respects, sacramental. They enable us, in a certain sense, to transcend the material world, move into the spiritual, and there abide in His saving presence. Here, as we bask in the light of His love, we're overwhelmed by the encounter and experience a profound sense of gratitude. "Lord, I am not worthy to have you enter under my roof" (Mt 8:8). It's precisely this gratitude, born of our participation in divine love, that is the inspiration of and motivation for diaconal ministry. Thus, the source of the deacon's diaconate, that which enables him to effectively incarnate Christ the Servant, is nothing other than intimate communion with Him. The interior life represents the place of inward encounter with Christ, without which a deacon is blind to the many exterior encounters with Christ that come his way each day. This inward encounter is what transforms the deacon's work from social work to ecclesial ministry, from a good thing to a saving reality.

In its broadest sense, the interior life is that inner place where we're alone with ourselves. It's the place of thought, imagination, deliberation, and choice. It's where we dream, pray, reflect, and meditate. It's where we discover God, ourselves, and others. It's the inner space where truth is grasped, goodness is acquired, beauty is appreciated, and love is born.

It's possible, with some reflection, to distinguish between the various dimensions of the interior life. There's the speculative, capable of intellectual thought; the moral, capable of choosing good or evil; and the spiritual, capable of intimacy with God and others. These are, of course, interrelated; in a certain sense, they interpenetrate one another, finding their nexus in our one person. Although they can be distinguished by their operations, they can't be separated without somehow obscuring the whole person.

While the interior life admits of all these dimensions, when we speak of it, we tend to speak of the spiritual dimension. Because of this, terms such as "interiority," "the inner life," and "the spiritual life" are often used synonymously in the Church's Tradition. We will follow this usage, with all of these terms referring to that inner place where we encounter Christ and seek intimate communion with Him.

The interior life is nonphysical and thus finds its exercises within the powers of the soul. To be human is to be a body/soul composite, and while the soul expresses the interior life, the body expresses the exterior life. These two aspects of our human nature are to be integrated. This integrity requires that for the interior life to be authentically lived, it must be expressed in the exterior life. This is nothing less than a corollary of faith and works. Accordingly, Saint James writes:

> What good is it, my brothers, if someone says he has faith but does not have works? Can that faith save him? If a brother or sister has nothing to wear and has no food for the day, and one of you says to them, "Go in peace, keep warm, and eat well," but you do not give them the necessities of the body, what good is it? So also faith of itself, if it does not have works, is dead. ... For just as a body without a spirit is dead, so also faith without works is dead. (Jas 2:14–17, 26)

Faith is an act of the interior life. For it to be realized and lived, it must be expressed in concrete acts consistent with what is professed. To do otherwise is to undermine its authenticity, calling into question whether that faith is truly held by the one professing it. Thus, if someone were to profess to be a faithful Catholic while at the same time being unfaithful to his wife, his profession of faith would be significantly undercut by his actions. Indeed, those actions that are inconsistent with the Faith would call into question whether he truly believes what he says he believes. He may deceive others, and even himself, but this inconsistency reveals his infidelity rather than his fidelity. Beyond this, if he freely and willingly engages in what he knows to be grave sin, he breaks communion with God and His Church. This is hardly the act of a faithful Catholic.

In many respects, the relationship between the interior and exterior life is sacramental. Properly understood, a sacramental, like the sacraments themselves, is a visible sign of invisible realities. The sign points to and makes present that which is hidden. Just as the body is the sacrament of the soul, the exterior life is a sacrament of the interior life. Without the body, the soul remains unknown, trapped in the realm of the spirit. It's precisely in and through the body that the soul enters the world and makes itself known and, equally importantly, comes to be known. Together, and only together, do body and soul express the whole person. In a similar manner, without the exterior life, the interior remains unknown. It's strictly in and through the exterior life that the interior life is revealed. Together, and only together, do they express the whole person.

To share such things as faith and spirituality, hopes and aspirations — indeed, to share our very selves in love — the interior life must transcend itself. This takes place only through the exterior life, expressed in concrete acts. Likewise, receiving another's faith and spirituality, hopes and aspirations — indeed, receiving their very selves in love — occurs first through our exterior life.

Our interior life is only accessed through the exterior life. This intrinsic relationship means that while we can explore the spirituality of the diaconate, we do so with the understanding that, as with faith and works, the interior life without the exterior life is dead.

THE DISTINCTIVENESS OF DIACONAL SPIRITUALITY

> *If you are what you should be, you will*
> *set the whole world ablaze!*
> **Attributed to Saint Catherine of Siena**

When the term "diaconal spirituality" is used in popular literature, its meaning is often assumed. The context of its usage implies the way a deacon draws close to Christ through such practices as *lectio divina,* various devotions, spiritual direction, frequent confession, and Eucharistic adoration. While all of these have great merit in cultivating the interior life, they don't in themselves constitute a diaconal spirituality. Instead, they are elements in the spirituality of a deacon. This may seem like a distinction without a difference, but upon closer examination, one can see that the difference is vast.

To be sure, a deacon may and should participate in these various devotions. Yet as we shall see, it's not the fact of his participation but rather how he participates that reflects his configuration to Christ the Servant. All of these devotions are a way of relating to God, and that relationship changed radically on the day of his ordination. Because he *is deacon*, because he has been indelibly marked as Christ the Servant, he now has the capacity to relate to God in a particular way, in a diaconal way. Since this relationship is contextualized as a gift of divine love outpoured, and since love cannot remain static, the essential characteristic and distinctive feature of diaconal spirituality is to grow in more intimate communion with Christ the Servant. In many respects, this defines not only diaconal spirituality but the deacon himself and becomes the source and strength of his ministry. It imbues his ministry with a particular quality — the quality of a servant who loves his Master tenderly.

The above definition of "diaconal spirituality," which forms the basis of our approach, uses the term in a collective sense. What is really meant is "diaconal spiritualities." There isn't any one way to grow in intimate communion with Christ the Servant, but many. Indeed, what is true of diaconal spiritualities and their associated devotions is true of all Catholic spiritualities. In his venerable work *Introduction to the Devout Life,* Saint Francis de Sales observes:

> When God created the world, He commanded each tree to bear fruit after its kind; and even so He bids Christians, the living trees of His Church, to bring forth fruits of devotion, each one according to his kind and vocation. A different exercise of devotion is required of each … and furthermore such practice must be modified according to the strength, the calling, and the duties of each individual.[1]

As we have already seen, intimate communion implies a relationship, and a relationship always implies the union of two or more distinct individuals. While Christ the Servant is a constant in the relationship, individual deacons are not. They represent a widely diverse group, and while they share many commonalities, the ways in which they encounter Christ and allow Him to accompany them on their vocational journeys will differ. Just as no one person can image God, so no one person can incar-

---

[1] Saint Francis de Sales, *Introduction to the Devout Life* (New York: Dover, 2009), 41.

nate Christ the Servant. The diversity of diaconal spiritualities reflects the diversity of men called to sacred service in the diaconate, and only together do they reveal Christ the Servant. In this way, they enable the ministry to permeate and penetrate all aspects of society. Thus, this work will consider that which is common to all diaconal spiritualities, along with ways to cultivate spiritual growth.

The uniqueness of diaconal spirituality, what sets it apart from other spiritualities, lies in the deacon's mystical identification with Christ the Servant. While all are called to serve by virtue of their Baptism, the deacon is called to be an icon of Christ the Servant, and in this respect, he acts in the person of that same Christ who came not to be served but to serve. This grounds diaconal spirituality in a specific kind of vocational relationship to God that begins as an unfulfilled calling, beckoning him to a life lived in sacred ecclesial service. This relationship is realized when his bishop says the prayer of ordination and lays hands upon him.[2] It continues throughout his life as he exercises his diaconal ministry. Because he *is deacon* by virtue of his ordination, his every act has the capacity to be diaconal. I say "has the capacity" because the deacon needs to be intentional about being a deacon. Ordination takes away neither the effects of original sin nor our free will, which, if it's truly free, maintains the capacity to sin. This intentionality is not limited to formal ministry per se, but applies to all aspects of his life, including and especially his relationships with his wife and his family. Indeed, he must first be a deacon to them as father and husband before he can be a deacon to others.

Diaconal spirituality in its many forms seeks to grow the deacon in the ways of perfection, enabling him to incarnate Christ the Servant more effectively. By sensitizing himself to God's presence in those he serves and responding in love, he

---

[2] The Diaconal Prayer of Ordination is found in the Appendix.

extends the hand of Christ to those in need. He is transformed in this process, since it's impossible to touch without being touched. To foster a greater intentionality within the exercise of his ministry, the deacon needs to foster that same intentionality within his interior life. He needs to seek Christ the Servant in all things and, in all things, discover Him anew.

THE IMPORTANCE OF EMPATHY

> *What does love look like? It has the hands to help others.*
> *It has the feet to hasten to the poor and needy. It has*
> *eyes to see misery and want. It has the ears to hear the*
> *sighs and sorrows of men. That is what love looks like.*
> **Saint Augustine,** *Confessions*

To serve others is to perceive a need in them and, to the extent possible, help them satisfy that need. If it's hunger, we give them food. If it's lack of faith, we proclaim the Good News. If it's loneliness, we give them company. Sometimes this means doing something; most times, it just means being present. In either case, our sensitivity to the needs of others, and consequently our desire to serve, arise not so much from a particular situation but first and foremost in our interiority. It's here that we feel another's pain, experiencing — albeit in a limited sense — his or her suffering. This diaconal characteristic has as its basis the virtue of empathy. Because empathy is critical to authentic Christian service, and because the diaconate is meant to exemplify service and inspire the faithful to serve, empathy is essential to an authentic diaconal spirituality. Without it, deacons cannot serve as Christ served. Without it, deacons cannot reach beyond their own limitations, providing the strength and consolation that those who suffer so desperately need.

In its most basic sense, empathy concerns the ability to recognize and enter into the experience of another. The term is grounded in the Greek prefix *em*, meaning "in," and the word *pathos*, meaning "suffering." This implies a deep personal sharing in another's hardship, such that the one empathizing experiences, in a certain sense, the hardship of the other. Empathy creates a bond between the two — the one accompanying the other as he carries his cross, reminding him that he is not alone and that someone cares. It is, in this respect, nothing less than an act of love.

In diaconal spirituality, it's important to recognize that the object of authentic empathy is not so much the suffering of the other but the other himself. Empathy is, at its core, an interpersonal reality. In this regard, by being empathetic, we accompany the sufferer through his or her sufferings. In a world dominated by positive action, this may seem feeble and ineffective. Sitting by a hospital bed, or spending time with someone with mental illness, or simply visiting a person who has lost a loved one may seem futile considered against the sickness, illness, or loss itself. However, a comforting presence — one that takes on the suffering of the other just by being there and listening quietly — brings a consolation that enables the sufferer not only to endure but to rise above the hardship, experiencing its redemptive value.

Jesus is the perfect model of empathy. By virtue of his Incarnation, He enters into the human condition with all of its sufferings. Not content to be a bystander dispassionately removed from human pathos, He takes on humanity's suffering through His Passion and death. Notice how Our Lord exercises this priestly aspect of His earthly ministry in a preeminently diaconal way.

In his book *The Heart of the Diaconate*, Deacon James Keating writes, "Empathy will only remain and deepen over many decades of ecclesial service if that empathy is sourced in Christ and restored in Him when human strength, interest and generosity lag."[3] While the fullness of God's grace subsists in the Catholic Church,[4] the finite Church cannot contain the infinite nature of God's grace. We see this in the many examples of the noble atheist whose selfless altruism inspires others. Nonetheless, it's often the case that love-of-man, without the corresponding love-of-God, renders the noble atheist incapable of sourcing his love beyond himself. True, his love is ultimately a limited participation in divine love, but it's rooted in a God he does not know, and so he cannot draw from Him, be inspired by Him, or be strengthened in Him.

However, when a deacon roots his spirituality and ministry in the love of Christ the Servant, he understands empathy in light of the Paschal Mystery and its personal promise of salvation. This broader spiritual approach enables him to appreciate empathy from Calvary to the empty tomb. He understands that empathy is often more about being at the foot of the Cross with the one who suffers, awaiting the Resurrection together, than about "doing something." This being with the sufferer is not the absence of ministry but, many times, the very best kind of ministry.

Like other spiritualities in the Church, diaconal spirituality doesn't arise in a vacuum. Rather, it's contextualized and enriched by a diverse spiritual, mystical, and ascetical tradition. When oriented to intimate communion with Christ the Servant, this tradition provides the necessary building blocks for developing and maintaining an authentically diaconal spirituality. With that in mind, we would do well to begin with one of the chief hallmarks of any spirituality: interior struggle. Treating interior struggle early in our consideration allows us to anticipate it and, when it rears

---

[3] James Keating, *The Heart of the Diaconate: Communion with the Servant Mysteries of Christ* (New York/Mahwah, NJ: Paulist Press, 2015), 7–8.

[4] *Lumen Gentium*, 8.

its ugly head, to cut it off by responding to God's grace.

STRUGGLE IN THE SPIRITUAL LIFE

Our interior life consists in beginning again and again.
Saint Josemaría Escrivá, *Christ Is Passing By*

The interior life is both a gift from God and an intentional response on our part. In the midst of life's demands, our response often requires great effort to sustain. As a result, if we're to progress in the spiritual life, we must consider as an essential component the struggles that accompany it. By struggles, I mean the ongoing work associated with picking up our cross and following Jesus. This includes the difficulties associated with various forms of prayer, meditations, devotions, or spiritual practices as they relate to the living out of our vocation. In many respects, to pray well is to struggle often. As the entire Tradition bears witness, the two go hand in hand.

To identify the spiritual life with spiritual struggle is to beg some deeper questions, the first of which concerns the reason for our struggle. Why do we struggle? Much of this has to do with the effects of what the Tradition calls "the three enemies of the soul": the world, the flesh, and the devil. These are the sources of our temptation, and they arise in a world tainted by original sin and still awaiting full redemption. They mirror Christ's temptations in the desert found in all three Synoptic Gospels (see Mt 4:1–11; Mk 1:12–13; Lk 4:1–13). The temptation of the world is represented by Satan's invitation to Our Lord to cast himself off the parapet, that of the flesh by the invitation to turn stones into bread, and that of the devil by the invitation to worship Satan. Elements of this triad can also be found in the Parable of the Sower (Mt 13:1–23; Mk 4:1–20; Lk 8:4–15) and in Saint Paul's Letter to the Ephesians, where he writes, "You were dead in your transgressions and sins in which you once lived following the age of this world, following the ruler of the power of the air, the spirit that is now at work in the disobedient. All of us once lived among them in the desires of our flesh, following the wishes of the flesh and the impulses, and we were by nature children of wrath, like the rest" (2:1–3).

THE UNHOLY TRINITY AND SLOTH

> *O Lord and Master of my life, grant me not a spirit*
> *of sloth, meddling, love of power, and idle talk. But*
> *give to me, your servant, a spirit of sober-mindedness,*
> *humility, patience, and love. Yes, O Lord and King,*
> *grant me to see my own faults and not to judge my*
> *brother, since you are blessed to the ages of ages. Amen.*
> **The Great Lenten Prayer of Saint Ephrem,**
> **Byzantine and Orthodox Traditions**

Reflecting on the above passages in light of the moral life, Tradition summarized these three enticements to sin, giving them the popular title the "Unholy Trinity." Accordingly, the French medieval philosopher Peter Abelard identified these three specific categories of temptation. Likewise, Saint Thomas Aquinas acknowledged their deadly nature in his *Summa Theologica.* Later, Saint John of the Cross identified these very same three as serious threats to the perfection of the soul. Although the definitions and treatments given by these thinkers vary slightly, they are, for the most part, quite consistent.

The "world" represents a willful indifference to the designs of God. This can be seen in the adoption of secular values in opposition to Christ and His Church. An example of the "world" is what Pope Saint John Paul II called "the culture of death," which includes the widespread acceptance of abortion, infanticide, and euthanasia. The "flesh" reflects the tendencies to gluttony and sexual immorality. These tendencies include our disordered passions and corrupt inclinations expressed in such evils as fornication, adultery, and homosexual acts. The "devil" represents himself — he is a real person, the chief fallen angel described by Saint John as "a liar and the father of lies" (Jn 8:44; see also 1 Jn 3:8). He and the rest of the fallen angels, known as demons, "prowl throughout the world seeking the ruin of souls."[5] Examples of the "devil" include such deadly practices as openness to temptation, participation in the occult, and satanism. When embraced or even passively tolerated, the Unholy Trinity have the real potential to erode our relationship with Christ the Servant, diminish significantly the effectiveness of our diaconal ministry and, if left unchecked, to contribute to the loss of our salvation.

These threats, often experienced in the form of strong temptations, represent the prime reason for struggle in the interior life. Other reasons include what Tradition calls the seven deadly (or capital) sins, which actually fall under the broader categories of the world, the flesh, and the devil. They are pride, greed, lust, envy, gluttony, wrath, and sloth. While treatment of these can be found in a number of good sources,[6] one of these capital sins stands out as particularly troublesome in the spiritual life: sloth.

Sloth, also known by its Latin name, *acedia*, refers to an interior struggle characterized by indifference to our religious duties and obligations. It's a kind of spiritual malaise where we fail to do the things we should. In this respect, it can easily become a sin of omission, especially when we cease to resist it. Writing in his *Pocket Catholic Dictionary*, the late Jesuit theologian Father John Hardon defined sloth as the "sluggishness of soul or boredom because of the exertion necessary for the performance of a

---

[5] Taken from the Prayer of Saint Michael.
[6] *Catechism of the Catholic Church*, 1866. Geoffrey Chaucer popularized them in the fourteenth century in his *Canterbury Tales*.

good work."[7] Sloth arises out of the interior desire to seek pleasure and avoid hardship, without regard to moral and spiritual implications. Sloth tempts us to often follow the path of least resistance, becoming only nominally active in the spiritual life and, in the extreme, religiously apathetic.

Sloth, which is as old as religion itself, was first identified by the Desert Father Evagrius of Pontus in the late fourth century. Writing in the early monastic tradition, he describes it as a monk's deep desire to leave his cell that arose out of an ongoing indifference to the Faith. Sloth in a monk easily led to futility in his monastic vocation. Saint Thomas Aquinas later describes it as "a sadness arising from the fact that the good is difficult."[8] In sloth, we become lukewarm to the promptings of the Holy Spirit, yielding to the weight of our lives and failing to source our strength in Christ the Servant.

While deacons are not monks, the same principles apply. We can allow ourselves to become slothful in the spiritual life, especially when it comes to things like our obligation to pray the Divine Office or to ensuring we have enough time for contemplative prayer. It's all too easy to rationalize away such spiritual exercises because of the demands of our vocation, without recognizing that unless we root ourselves in these practices, we cannot truly fulfill that vocation. In much the same way that respiration requires for its success a twofold act — breathing in and breathing out — so too does the Christian life. Through the cultivation of the spiritual life, we breathe in the love of God and breathe out that same love of God, now transformed in us, to those we serve. If we simply breathe in and stop, we will inevitably die. Likewise, if we simply breathe out and stop, we will also perish. The movement from interiority to exteriority and back again reveals a wholesome integrity that gives life to us and,

---

[7] John Hardon, *Pocket Catholic Dictionary* (New York: Doubleday, 1980), 60–61.
[8] Thomas Aquinas, *Summa Theologica*, II-II, q.35, a.1.

through us, to those we serve.

Although sloth is often associated with inactivity, there is a type of sloth that masks itself in a flurry of actions unrelated to the interior life. As Evagrius points out, we may well be busy with a great many things, even holy things, and still be slothful. This happens when we busy ourselves with exterior acts of piety as a way to avoid the much harder work associated with cultivating the interior life. The lack of interiority associated with exterior acts leaves those acts, as we have already seen, sterile and lifeless. Because we fail to grow in intimacy with Christ the Servant through constancy in the interior life, sloth leads to a cold, depersonalized ministry in which, instead of relating to those we serve, we merely function. As a consequence of our failure to encounter Jesus in the world within us, we're rendered incapable of recognizing Him in the world around us. This condition, and its after-effect, is poetically captured in the Book of Proverbs and its consideration of a slothful person or "sluggard." The sacred author writes:

I passed by the field of a sluggard,
  by the vineyard of one with no sense;
It was all overgrown with thistles;
    its surface was covered with nettles,
    and its stone wall broken down.
As I gazed at it, I reflected;
    I saw and learned a lesson:
A little sleep, a little slumber,
    a little folding of the arms to rest —
Then poverty will come upon you like a robber,
    and want like a brigand. (24:30–34)

In examining the struggles associated with the interior life, we've considered the most common kinds of difficulties. However, if we're not careful, we risk passing over that which is so obvious as to be missed. In its consideration of the battle of prayer, the *Catechism* focuses in this passage on the object of that battle:

> Prayer is both a gift of grace and a determined response on our part. It always presupposes effort. The great figures of prayer of the Old Covenant before Christ, as well as the Mother of God, the saints, and he himself, all teach us this: prayer is a battle. Against whom? Against ourselves and against the wiles of the tempter who does all he can to turn man away from prayer, away from union with God. We pray as we live, because we live as we pray. If we do not want to act habitually according to the Spirit of Christ, neither can we pray habitually in his name. The "spiritual battle" of the Christian's new life is inseparable from the battle of prayer. (2725)

Sometimes, that which is right in front of us is most hidden. With regard to the interior life, we ourselves are the only constant element in every single one of our struggles. Our struggles with the Unholy Trinity and sloth are made possible only by our willingness to accept them, to appropriate them, to make them our own. True, we're surrounded by things and persons that constantly tempt us, but grace makes it possible not only to resist, but use these very same temptations as spiritual springboards to perfection. By not recognizing ourselves as the origin of our interior struggles, we look away from both the source of the problem and the solution.

GRACE IS THE REMEDY

Never give up prayer, and should you find dryness and difficulty, persevere in it for this very reason. God often desires to see what love your soul has,

> *and love is not tried by ease and satisfaction.*
> **Saint John of the Cross, *Special Counsels:***
> ***Degrees of Perfection, no. 9***

Grace is nothing less than supernatural help, an expression of divine love. To detach love from grace is to depersonalize the gift and, by extension, the Giver. Grace is not so much something given as Someone encountered in an intimate way. It is Christ the Servant, meeting us on the road to Calvary, helping us to carry our cross, enabling us to endure our sufferings and, in the end, to bask in the light of our own resurrection.

This divine love, given to us in grace to engage in the struggles of the interior life, can never be understated. God desires us more than we can ever desire Him. He seeks us out more than we seek Him. God's absolute and unconditional love, and the grace that flows from it, is most fully expressed in the Passion, Death, and Resurrection of His Son. Jesus says, "No one has greater love than this, to lay down one's life for one's friends" (Jn 15:13).

Our Lord gives himself to us, and in this very giving He offers us the grace necessary to overcome our struggles. Because his love is unconditional, there's nothing we can do to make Him love us more and nothing we can do to make Him love us less. He is love through and through. Knowing this, we can recognize that it's a grand lie of Satan that we must be good to allow God to draw close to us. As Saint Paul observes, "God proves his love for us in that while we were still sinners Christ died for us" (Rom 5:8). We often buy into Satan's lie because we superimpose the frailties of human love over God's love rather than allowing God's love to be the measure of our love. God's love is meant to purify our love so that our love reflects, albeit in a human way, His love.

Since it's an expression of divine love, grace is completely unmerited. There's absolutely nothing we can do to earn it. It's a gratuitous gift from God just because He's God and we're our-selves. That's it. God's love for us is grounded not in what we do but simply in our very being, in the pure and simple fact that we exist in His image. If this seems rather abstract, think of the love a father has for his son. Should the son, as he grows, engage in acts the father disapproves of, such disapproval does not di-minish the love he has for his son. This is nothing less than the principle of loving the sinner and hating the sin. The father sees beyond his son's acts to the babe he held long ago, to the boy he raised, to the man that boy has become. The father loves the son for who he is, and it's because of this love that he hates what his son's sins do to him and to others around him. Nonetheless, the father can no more abandon his son than he can abandon himself. In this respect, authentic love, be it divine or human, is constant, regardless of the acts of the beloved. This is not to say that human love has the same power as divine love, only that human love, when rooted in God's love, has power beyond itself. In this respect, human love at its best is a participation in and an expression of divine love.

SURRENDER IS ABANDONMENT

> *Love consumes us only in the measure*
> *of our self-surrender.*
> **Saint Thérèse of Lisieux,** *The Story of a Soul*

If we accept God's help, we accept a kind of divine embrace. We allow Jesus to place His arms around us, steadying us when we falter, picking us up when we collapse, and carrying us when we're exhausted. As we do so, His strength becomes our strength, and His love becomes our love, diminishing the interior struggle and rendering our diaconal ministry more effective. For us to receive this divine help requires one thing and one thing only:

that we surrender to Christ the Servant. It's letting go and letting God, not just in situations that exceed our strength but eventually in all things. Surrender doesn't mean that we step out of the way and passively hope God steps in; it means that we allow Him to work in and through us, transforming us in the process. Implicit in this surrender is the recognition that we simply can't make it to our eternal destiny without Him. Christ the Servant fills a space within the heart of a deacon that no one else can fill — such that without Our Lord, we're incomplete and life loses its purpose and meaning.

My spiritual director from many years ago used to tell me that God can do anything He wants with me, if I let Him. Since in authentic love, the lover never forces himself on the beloved, God's love, expressed in grace, is never imposed upon us, but is instead offered as a free invitation. He extends His hand to us, but it's up to us to grasp it. As Christians, and particularly in our vocation to the diaconate, we're called to surrender to and suffer the presence of Christ in the moment. While grace may not necessarily make this easy, it will always make it possible. In surrendering, we begin to see ourselves more clearly for who we are and to see the key role we play in our own struggle.

Surrender, which is far more a lifelong process than a single event, begins with a fundamental recognition that God is God and we're not. In giving God our very selves, we're giving Him not so much something that's exclusively ours as that which is rightfully His. In faithfully living out our diaconate, we're not simply returning the gift we've received but offering our own unique gift to Him in return. This is an act of sincere gratitude.

Catholic Tradition has long recognized both grace as a remedy for our struggles and our need to continually surrender. This is particularly evident in the Sacrament of Reconciliation. There, instead of just asking for the forgiveness of sins as though they are external to us, we say, "Bless me Father, for

I have sinned." The "me" in this request is a recognition of that obvious yet hidden truth: that the struggle in the interior life is first and foremost a struggle within us and by us. Consequently, it's not so much the Unholy Trinity that ensnares us but we who allow the Unholy Trinity to do so. We're the authors of our own sins, and then, because the interior struggle arises out of a resistance to grace, we're the authors of our own struggles. True, some struggles come as a result of our fallen nature or the sins of others forced upon us, but these too can be addressed by grace. We don't author these in the same sense and thus are not always responsible for them before God. Still, we're responsible for the extent to which we resist the grace offered to oppose these struggles. Recognizing and acknowledging this fundamental truth of the interior life allows us to take hold of it in a healthy way; it enables us to seek the necessary spiritual remedies and thereby grow in perfection.

STRUGGLE AS A WAY OF PERFECTION

> *Without the burden of afflictions, it is impossible*
> *to reach the height of grace. The gift of grace*
> *increases as the struggle increases.*
> **Saint Rose of Lima, Office of Readings, August 23**

To those unfamiliar with the spiritual and mystical traditions, struggles may seem antithetical to growth in holiness. After all, aren't those who have grown in perfection more at peace within themselves? While it's certainly true that the interior life can provide a certain peace, this peace doesn't mean the absence of struggle, at least not this side of heaven.

While we're on earth, regardless of our spiritual state, we will struggle to a greater or lesser degree. This is nothing less than the lifelong battle between love-of-God and love-of-self due to the effects of original sin and our own personal sins. We can no more omit this struggle from our salvation than the Cross could be omitted from the Resurrection. Indeed, just as it was precisely in and through the Cross that Jesus rose from the dead, opening up to us the gates to eternal life, it is precisely in and through our struggles that we will experience the fruit of Christ's redemption. This isn't at all to suggest that our struggles merit our salvation. Regardless of what we do — no matter how great, no matter how noble — we're radically incapable of saving ourselves. This attitude that our works can earn our salvation, which is a form of Pelagianism, has been consistently condemned by the Church as heretical. It's only by responding to the grace merited for us by Jesus' own struggle (His Passion and death) that we're rendered capable of uniting our struggle with His and, in this way, working out our salvation with fear and trembling (see Phil 2:12).

The saints throughout the whole of the Catholic spiritual and mystical tradition have borne witness to this "working out." When we read the unvarnished lives of the saints, we discover that precisely this struggle, often described as a kind of spiritual dryness, marked much of their lives. Indeed, the entire canon of saints is replete with men and women who struggled in the pursuit of spiritual perfection. While many, such as Saint Francis of Assisi, Saint Anthony Claret, Saint Teresa of Ávila, and Saint John of the Cross, were and are well known, many others, such as Saint Hilarion, Saint Louise de Marillac, Saint Mary Magdalene de Pazzi, and Saint Josepha Rossello, are lesser known. Perhaps one of the struggles best known today is that of the late nineteenth-century French Carmelite nun Saint Thérèse of Lisieux. In her autobiography titled *The Story of a Soul*, she writes:

> I must tell you about my retreat for [religious] profession. Far from experiencing any consolation, complete aridity — desolation, almost — was my lot. Jesus was

asleep in my little boat as usual. How rarely souls let Him sleep peacefully within them. Their agitation and all their requests have so tired out the Good Master that He is only too glad to enjoy the rest I offer Him. I do not suppose He will wake up until my eternal retreat, but instead of making me sad, it makes me very happy. Such an attitude of mind proves that I am far from being a saint. I should not rejoice in my aridity, but rather consider it as the result of lack of fervor and fidelity, while the fact that I often fall asleep during meditation or while making my thanksgiving should appall me. Well, I am not appalled; I bear in mind that little children are just as pleasing to their parents asleep as awake, that doctors put their patients to sleep while they perform operations, and that after all, "the Lord knows our frame. He remembers that we are but dust."[9]

In his famous *Spiritual Exercises*, Saint Ignatius of Loyola spoke of this struggle in terms of consolation and desolation. Consolation arises when prayer is tranquil, blissful, and satisfying. This may happen either as a reward for our fidelity or as a gratuitous gift from God. Similarly, desolation in prayer often comes as a means to purify us from our attachments. If we allow it, desolation can strengthen us by reminding us of our utter dependence on the grace of God. This "reminder" is a great gift, though in the midst of particularly intense struggles, it may seem more like a curse. Nowhere is this more beautifully illustrated than by Saint Paul in his Second Letter to the Corinthians, where he speaks of his personal struggle as a "thorn in [his] flesh." He writes:

> Three times I begged the Lord about this, that it might leave me, but he said to me, "My grace is sufficient for

---

[9] Thérèse of Lisieux, *The Story of a Soul* (New York: Dover, 2008), 115.

you, for power is made perfect in weakness." I will rather boast most gladly of my weaknesses, in order that the power of Christ may dwell with me. Therefore, I am content with weaknesses, insults, hardships, persecutions, and constraints, for the sake of Christ; for when I am weak, then I am strong. (12:8–10)

Whereas consolation inspires us to persevere in prayer and devotion, desolation refines us in the fire and allows the greatest progress in the spiritual life. Anyone can pray, fulfill obligations, and serve others when it's easy. What sacrifice is there in that? However, when we pray, fulfill our obligations, and serve others in the midst of desolation, we demonstrate our willingness to "die" for Christ. This death-to-self is an expression of love, an act of gratitude in response to the great gifts we've already received. Saint Pio of Pietrelcina often observed that the life of a Christian is nothing but a perpetual struggle against self. There is, he taught, no flowering of the soul except at the price of pain.

When accomplished in desolation, our prayers, the fulfilment of our obligations, and indeed our diaconal service are far more powerful than those very same acts done in consolation. As Saint John Eudes reminds us, "You can advance farther in grace in one hour during this time of affliction than in many days during a time of consolation." Similarly, Saint Francis de Sales writes:

Our actions are like roses, which when fresh have more beauty but when dry have more strength and sweetness. In like manner, our works performed with tenderness of heart are more agreeable to ourselves — to ourselves, I say, who regard only our own satisfaction. Yet when performed in times of dryness, they possess more sweetness and become more precious in the sight of God.[10]

Desolation provides us with unique opportunities to anchor our love in Christ the Servant by uniting our struggles with His timeless, eternal sacrifice. If we see them in faith, our struggles become grace-filled moments enabling us to live out our vocations in fidelity to the will of God. They provide occasions to "offer up" our imperfect sacrifices and, through Him, make them perfect, which transforms us in the process. All of this, when done in a state of grace, leads to greater intimacy with Our Lord.

Understood this way, struggle marks a vitality rather than a failure in the spiritual life. Struggle is our effort, united with and inspired by grace, to overcome our sinful ways and seek a life of virtue and sanctity, imperfect as it may be. Struggle, therefore, deserves a place at the beginning of any consideration of Catholic spirituality. This is particularly true for those new to the interior life, as it often begins with a "honeymoon" period, inevitably followed by a dive into the spiritual abyss. Saint Philip Neri counsels, "As a rule, people who aim at a spiritual life begin with the sweet and afterward pass on to the bitter. So now, away with all tepidity, off with that mask of yours, carry your cross, don't leave it to carry you."[11]

While struggle in the interior life has its place, we should neither deliberately seek it nor merely tolerate it when it could be remedied. This is not to deny its redemptive value; however, we have equal responsibility to diminish our struggles when possible so that what remains can be taken up in the interior life. God never gives us more than we can handle, but sometimes we do. If, for example we're struggling in prayer because we're in a noisy place, then instead of offering it up, we should move. That's our

---

[10] Francis de Sales, *The Consoling Thoughts of St. Francis de Sales*, ed. Rev. Père Huguet (Dublin: M. H. Gill and Sons, 1877), 221.

[11] Quoted in Jill Haak Adels, ed., *The Wisdom of the Saints* (New York: Oxford University Press, 1987), 190.

first responsibility. If we're unable to move, then by all means, we should offer it up. All too often, we impose a pseudo-cross upon ourselves. We may do this for many reasons, sometimes because of scrupulosity and other times because the pseudo-cross diverts us from our real cross. To continue with this example, when the actual reason we're praying in a noisy place is because we'd rather not face God in the silence of our hearts, prayer becomes an avoidance rather than an encounter.

For those spiritual struggles we can't avoid, the best remedy is perseverance, an act of fidelity to the God who created us out of love and saved us while we were yet sinners. In its most basic sense, perseverance is tenacity in the interior life despite difficulties. It's the persistence necessary, this side of heaven, to work through the challenges that impede us from intimate communion with Christ the Servant. In this regard, perseverance doesn't simply consist of passively enduring our struggles, much as we might hunker down in the midst of a terrible storm. Instead, perseverance consists of actively engaging in the struggle by applying a spiritual remedy so that the very struggle becomes a means to holiness. Fortunately, the saints and mystics of the Church who fought these very same battles and, with grace, won have left us a rich inheritance from which we can learn. In his book *Christ Is Passing By*, Saint Josemaría Escrivá observes:

A Christian's struggle must be unceasing, for interior life consists in beginning and beginning again. This prevents us from proudly thinking that we are perfect already. It's inevitable that we should meet difficulties on our way. If we did not come up against obstacles, we would not be creatures of flesh and blood. We will always have passions which pull us downwards; we will always have to defend ourselves against more or less self-defeating urges.[12]

Beyond the call for divine help, which should be constant, what else can we do in the midst of interior struggle? If we're struggling with dryness in the spiritual life, Saint Jane Frances de Chantal assures us that "the great method of prayer is to have none. If, in going to prayer, one can form in oneself a pure capacity for receiving the Spirit of God, that will suffice for all method."[13] This wise advice speaks not to the prayer itself but to our interior disposition while praying. It reminds us that at its most fundamental level, prayer is a question not of "what" but of "whom," guiding us to the One to whom our prayers are directed. This is made possible when we adopt an inner attitude of receptivity, despite the often frenetic pace of our lives. It requires us, to the extent possible, to slow down and take a breath before prayer. It obliges us to calm ourselves, preparing not so much to speak to God but to hear him, not so much to do something but to be with Him.

Notice here that prayer, and indeed all spiritual works, are not ends in themselves. We don't pray for prayer's sake any more than we converse for conversation's sake. Like conversation, prayer mediates and allows for an encounter with the other; the absence of this encounter robs prayer of its very purpose — interpersonal communion. It's all too easy to lose sight of this and, feeling our prayers as useless, to stop praying. Saint Alphonsus Liguori's counsel is particularly helpful here:

> This, then, is your answer whenever you feel tempted to stop praying because it seems to be a waste of time: "I am here to please God." The measure of prayer isn't

---

[12] Josemaría Escrivá, *Christ Is Passing By* (New York: Scepter, 2002), no. 75.

[13] Francis de Sales and Jane de Chantal, *Letters of Spiritual Direction*, ed. Wendy M. Wright and Joseph F. Power, trans. Péronne Marie Thibert (New York: Paulist Press, 1988), 51.

whether it pleases us, but whether it pleases God; and our willingness to persevere for His glory will, in turn, aid our own spiritual growth.[14]

Because we're body/soul composites, good spiritual advice should always be accompanied by equally good practical advice. When we struggle, it's often helpful to keep our prayers short and simple. After all, God already knows the complexities of our hearts better than we do. We don't need to convince Him of our concerns with compelling arguments; we only need appeal to Him from the depths of our hearts with sincerity. When his spiritual directees were dry as dust in prayer, Saint Paul of the Cross counseled them not to quit and to keep going using short prayers.

Struggles in the interior life, particularly when they're experienced as dryness, can also be dealt with effectively through Eucharistic adoration. In prayer, as noted earlier, we needn't have the words but simply the willingness to sit quietly with Him. Silence before the Blessed Sacrament can have a consoling effect, especially when it's focused on the Real Presence. Simply acknowledging Jesus fully present — Body, Blood, Soul, and Divinity — has a grace in itself and is well worth the effort. In a similar sense, realize that when we pray, we always do so in the presence of our guardian angel. Saint John Vianney reminds us that "if you find it impossible to pray, hide behind your good angel, and charge him to pray in your stead."[15]

---

[14] Quoted in Joseph M. Esper, *Saintly Solutions to Life's Common Problems* (Manchester, NH: Sophia Institute Press, 2001), 287.

[15] Ibid.

Chapter Two
The Necessity of Abandonment

Imagine that this Lord himself is at your side and see how lovingly and how humbly He is teaching you — and, believe me, you should stay with so good a Friend for as long as you can before you leave Him. If you become accustomed to having Him at your side, and if He sees that you love Him to be there and are always trying to please Him, you will never be able to send Him away, nor will He ever fail you. He will help you in all your trials and you will have Him everywhere. Do you think it's a small thing to have such a Friend as that beside you?

Saint Teresa of Ávila, *The Way of Perfection*

The entire purpose of the Christian life is intimate communion with Jesus Christ. This communion, which grows as we progress in the interior life, is critical to the identity and mission of all Christians. By virtue of his ordination to the diaconate, the deacon's sense of who he is and what he is called to do gains a new intensity and direction. The manner in which the newly ordained relates to Our Lord and His Church means that his life must now bear witness, in an exemplary way, to Christ the Servant. This new specificity, grounded in Baptism, strengthened in Confirmation, purified in Reconciliation, and nourished in the Eucharist, builds upon his earlier sacramental identity; and his progressive sanctification provides the deacon with the supernatural graces so necessary to fulfill his sacred vocation. Simply put, for the deacon to respond to God's call effectively, he must continually appropriate and unfold the graces already received at his ordination. The ongoing reception of these graces requires a willingness to cultivate the interior life as though it were his first task, his last task, and his only task.

Divine abandonment means surrendering our lives to God's will. The term "surrender," as it relates to abandonment, is quite instructive: in its broadest sense, it means to stop fighting. Surrender presupposes and reveals the interior battle we all experience as a result of our fallen yet redeemed natures. Though Baptism freed us from original sin and incorporated us into the Church, concupiscence — that is, the tendency to sin — remains. To abandon ourselves to the divine will is to gain strength for the battle within us: the battle between selflessness and selfishness, the battle between virtue and vice, the battle between good and evil. Of course, this battle will not end until we draw our last breath. Still, by abandoning ourselves to the will of God, we can, with grace, not only survive this battle but triumph.

Surrender isn't so much an event as a lifelong process often characterized by interior conflict. Like struggle, far from being a sign of failure, inner conflict is a hallmark of the spiritual life. Applied to abandonment, inner conflict typically occurs in two stages paralleling the two powers of the soul — the intellect and the will. The intellect first perceives a truth and the need to correspond to it by changing our way of life. In the exercise of our conscience, we know something is wrong and realize that, to be right with God and at peace within ourselves, we need to reform. But the desire to reform is only the first stage of the battle. It's a kind of spiritual awakening on the intellectual level, a perception of the difference between what is good and how we have been living. Though this intellectual conflict is good because it admits our need to move beyond where we are to a better place with God, it's not enough by itself.

To advance toward divine abandonment, we must take up the second stage, that of the will. Whereas the intellect seeks the truth, the will, which is associated with specific concrete acts, seeks the good. For example, in order to be faithful to what we believe, we must maintain custody of the tongue. Gossip among Christians, and especially among clergy, is always wrong. When we gossip, especially when it becomes calumny, we sin; and when we sin, we weaken our relationship with God. Our intellects grasp this truth, and our consciences are formed by it. However, if we stop at this intellectual stage and never incorporate this truth into our will and actions — such that we persist in doing evil — it will eat us from the inside out. Alignment between the intellect and the will, as these are shaped by God's revelation to us regarding how we are to grow in grace and perfection in Him, allows us to experience integrity and, as a direct result, to live in bold confidence.

Of course, the movement from the intellect to the will requires considerable work, often characterized by fits and starts. This is precisely why it's often described as a battle. By ourselves, we find this movement almost impossible, but with grace, all things are possible. Grace, God's supernatural help, enables us to move our interior conflicts, perhaps ever so slowly at first, from the intellect to the will. It allows us to participate with Him such that we cooperate in our own salvation (see Phil 2:12) and, through our life and ministry, in the salvation of others. In this sense, interior conflict becomes the "place" of purification and sanctification. It's nothing less than our cross leading to our resurrection. Despite the ongoing frustrations associated with this conflict, it's part and parcel of the surrender necessary to abandon ourselves to the divine will.

Properly understood, surrender is grounded in a response to divine love already received. When we grow in awareness of how much God loves us, we're overwhelmed with joy and, in gratitude, want to respond to Him in kind. This means allowing His will to shape and direct our desires and plans. In this respect, we never lose our will, never become mere automatons in the hands of God, but instead permit His revelation of a personal love in Christ to purify and perfect our will. As a result, our wills, indeed our entire lives, become what they should be, and in this slow and sometimes arduous process, we paradoxically discover who we really are and what we're really called to do.

As both the Scriptures and Tradition attest, there's no way to cultivate the interior life and grow in intimate communion without some form of divine abandonment. We need only recall the lives of Abraham, Moses, Job, and the prophets in the Old Testament; likewise, in the New Testament, we remember the Blessed Virgin Mary, John the Baptist, Peter, and the other apostles. Of course, the greatest example of abandonment is Jesus Christ. His entire life, death, and resurrection were the perfect example of surrender to the Father's will. Indeed, He was quite explicit about this when He said to His apostles, "I came down from heaven not to do my own will but the will of the one who sent me" (Jn 6:38).

His abandonment didn't waver, despite the trial that would ensue. During the agony in the Garden of Gethsemane, Jesus prayed, "Father, if you are willing, take this cup away from me; still, not my will but yours be done" (Lk 22:42). Jesus' words and His subsequent Passion reveal that abandonment to the divine will carries with it personal hardship. Consider the trials of Job (see Jb 1:11), or the sword that pierced Mary's heart (Lk 2:35), or Peter's martyrdom (Jn 21:18–19). Jesus himself knew well this conflict as He spread His arms on the Cross for us. All of these examples illustrate that there's a real cost associated with abandonment, for it is, in its most fundamental sense, a response to Jesus' invitation "Whoever wishes to come after me must deny himself, take up his cross, and follow me" (Mt 16:24). Abandonment, properly understood, is not a purely human effort to follow Jesus, but rather a grace-filled response to a God who has already drawn close to us.

Like the Scriptures, the Tradition is replete with saints and mystics abandoning themselves to the divine will amid great struggles. Certainly one of the most noteworthy is Saint Augustine of Hippo, who lived in the late third and early fourth centuries. His was a long and arduous process, which he describes in Book Eight of his *Confessions*. At a critical point in his conversion, he admits to himself, "I had now found the priceless pearl and I ought to have sold all that I had and bought it — yet I hesitated."[1]

In this, the great saint reveals an internal battle of two wills — one pulling him to divine abandonment and the other pulling him to his own sinful desires. These are not literally two distinct wills, but a figurative way of saying that his will is torn between two distinct alternatives. The conflict between these two "wills" intensifies Augustine's perception of his own sinfulness. Praying, he says to God, "And now you set me face to face with myself,

---

[1] Augustine, *Confessions* (New York: Penguin Books, 1960), bk. 8, chap. 1.

that I might see how ugly I was, and how crooked and sordid, bespotted and ulcerous. And I looked and I loathed myself."[2]

In the midst of this struggle, Augustine sees with ever-greater clarity the impact of his sins and realizes he must repent. Still, there is a great chasm between his knowing what he must do (in his intellect) and his actually doing it — that is, choosing with his will to follow his intellect. Such a movement means a radical conversion — giving up the many sins that up to this point have defined his life. In deep anguish and near despair, he walks with his friend Alypius into a courtyard. Augustine's struggle at this point has become so intense that Alypius, unable to console him, leaves his friend in solitude, while remaining at a distance. Shortly thereafter, Augustine falls to the ground, sobbing uncontrollably. In his anguish, using the words of the psalmist, he cries out, "How long, O Lord?" Of this moment, Augustine later reflects, "I was saying these things and weeping in the most bitter contrition of my heart, when suddenly I heard the voice of a boy or a girl (I know not which) — coming from the neighboring house, chanting over and over again. 'Pick it up, read it; pick it up, read it.'"[3]

Returning to Alypius, Augustine takes up the Scriptures and randomly opens to Saint Paul's Letter to the Romans. There he reads, "Let us conduct ourselves properly as in the day, not in orgies and drunkenness, not in promiscuity and licentiousness, not in rivalry and jealousy" (Rom 13:13). These very sins describe his struggle with uncanny accuracy. Later he says of this moment, "I wanted to read no further, nor did I need to. For instantly, as the sentence ended, there was infused in my heart something like the light of full certainty and all the gloom of doubt vanished away."[4]

---

[2] Ibid., bk. 8, chap. 7.
[3] Ibid., bk. 8, chap. 12.
[4] Ibid.

AWARENESS OF THE EVER-PRESENT GOD

God is everywhere … and the fullness of His majesty
is present even in hidden and secret places.
Cyprian of Carthage, ***Treatise on the Lord's Prayer***

The work of the eighteenth-century French Jesuit Jean-Pierre de Caussade provides a starting point for our consideration of abandonment as it applies to diaconal spirituality. Because de Caussade's work speaks of surrender to God as its core element, it illustrates an essential first step in all spiritualities, including that of the diaconate. This step establishes the boundaries in the relationship with an indispensable twofold truth — namely, that God is God, and we're not. This recognition, which is far more a lifetime coming-to-know than a single event, gives rise to the realization that without union with Him, we're incomplete and our lives lack true meaning and purpose. As Saint Thomas Aquinas writes, "The will's desire is satisfied by the divine good alone as its last end."[5] To put it another way, only God can satisfy our deepest longing and, in doing so, enable us to live in eternal happiness.

Surrender to God represents the first step to union with Him, for it is an act of love. It represents an abandonment of the will that paradoxically enables us to more fully appropriate and refine that will. This truth enabled Saint Augustine to boldly proclaim, "Love God and do what you will."[6] Augustine understood well that if we truly love God, if we abandon our will to His, our entire lives will be transformed. This bond of love means that His desires become our desires, His choices become our choices, and His mission becomes our mission. Here, we don't lose our identity but instead discover it, becoming more fully who we are. Divine love, when accepted and internalized, makes possible an incarnation of sorts,

---

[5] Thomas Aquinas, *Summa contra Gentiles*, b.3, c.88, a.3.
[6] Augustine, *Sermon 7 on 1 John*, 8.

enabling us as deacons to act in the person of Christ the Servant.

Jean-Pierre de Caussade was born in southern France in 1675, more than a century and a half after the Protestant Reformation. It was the time of the Catholic Counter-Reformation, which brought with it not only the establishment of the seminary system and the reform of clerical life but a spiritual revival. Preceding de Caussade in the spiritual revival were such towering figures as Philip Neri, Francis de Sales, Jane Frances de Chantal, Ignatius of Loyola, Teresa of Ávila, and John of the Cross. Notable in this movement was a growing understanding that holiness is not limited to priestly and religious life, but includes the lay faithful as well. While this understanding did not come to full fruition until the Second Vatican Council's universal call to holiness, it nonetheless had its roots in the spiritual approaches of the sixteenth and seventeenth centuries, of which de Caussade would have been a beneficiary. He writes:

> Therefore, do I preach abandonment, and not any particular state. Every state in which souls are placed by Your grace is the same to me. I teach a general method by which all can attain the state which You have marked out for them. I do not exact more than the will to abandon themselves to Your guidance. You will make them arrive infallibly at the state which is best for them. It's faith that I preach; abandonment, confidence, and faith; the will to be subject to, and to be the tool of the divine action, and to believe that at every moment this action is working in every circumstance, provided that the soul has more or less good-will.[7]

We know relatively little of de Caussade's life. At the age of eigh-

---

[7] Jean-Pierre de Caussade, *Abandonment to Divine Providence*, ed. H. Ramière (St. Louis: B. Herder, 1921), 36.

teen, he entered the Society of Jesus. Ordained to the priesthood in 1704, he was later sent to Toulouse, where he obtained a doctorate in theology. De Caussade became proficient in Greek, Latin, and philosophy, along with physics. Some years later, he became the spiritual director to the Visitation Sisters in Nancy. Spiritual writings ascribed to de Caussade were first published after his death by fellow Jesuit Henri Ramière in 1861 under the title *L'abandon à la Providence divine* (*Abandonment to Divine Providence*). The work is said to be a compilation of letters sent to the sisters in his absence. While recent scholarship has questioned de Caussade's authorship, this in no way undermines the work's great value as a spiritual classic.

While de Caussade's work will be our starting point, it will not be given a full synopsis. It will instead act as an inspiration and a guide. Although there are a great many universals found in de Caussade's thought, he was writing in a particular time to a particular audience. In this respect, a number of nuances proper to eighteenth-century Catholicism will not apply to us today, at least not directly. What I hope to do here instead, as elsewhere in this work, is to take these universals and apply them to the diaconate as it exists today. Should the reader wish a more complete presentation of *Abandonment to Divine Providence*, he should read the work in its entirety.

De Caussade echoes much of the spiritual tradition of his time by acknowledging that God continues to reveal himself — though, unlike the public Revelations in the apostolic age that belong to the Sacred Deposit of Faith, the revelations of which de Caussade speaks are directed to individuals. These personal revelations deepen and enrich what God has already revealed in the Church's foundation, in much the same way as spousal love is deepened and enriched over time. As the years progress, spouses don't discover someone new; rather, through the triumphs and tragedies of life, they grow to understand and appreciate the other more deeply. In a similar manner, personal revelations unfold what God has already revealed in a particular moment to an individual. They are meant to touch the believer concretely in his life as he lives out the Faith, helping him to personally appropriate and integrate the Faith into his life. Put more figuratively, the unfolding of personal revelation allows the Faith to move between the head and the heart. I say "between" the head and heart because the head and heart set up a dialectic of sorts, a kind of back-and-forth. The Faith is first understood (head) and then personally appropriated (heart); but then the heart desires more because love desires more, and so it seeks to understand more.

All of this is predicated on the understanding that God's Revelation is a sharing not merely of His plan of salvation, but of His very self. More to the point, it's an offer of divine love, and we simply cannot love what we don't understand. This means the whole person, head and heart, is united in saying yes to the offer of divine love, which is far more a process than an event. Personal revelations find their authenticity and legitimacy when they are consistent with Divine Revelation as expressed in Sacred Scripture and interpreted by the Church. Depending on the gravity of such revelations, they may need to be discussed with a spiritual director, confessor, spouse, or trusted confidant. As Saint John warns, "Beloved, do not believe every spirit but test the spirits to see whether they belong to God, because many false prophets have gone out into the world" (1 Jn 4:1).

GOD'S HIDDEN OPERATIONS

Where can I go from your spirit?
From your presence, where can I flee?
If I ascend to the heavens, you are there;
if I lie down in Sheol, there you are.
Psalm 139:7–8

De Caussade speaks of these personal revelations as God's "hidden operations." Embedded in the very fabric of our lives — in the people we meet, in the situations we encounter — God speaks to us. To say that "God speaks" isn't to suggest an audible voice from heaven. Though this is certainly not beyond His power, divine locutions are not His typical mode of communication. Instead, God generally speaks to the soul with a voice that only the soul can hear. This "divine voice" arises not so much in silence itself, but in the silence that follows prayerful meditation and reflection on the events of our lives. These events are not necessarily major turning points; more often than not, they are the simple comings and goings of our day that — and this is important — give rise to certain duties.

This said, before we get ahead of ourselves, it will be necessary to consider how the Church understands the presence of God.

The Church has long taught that, like omniscience and omnipotence, omnipresence is a divine attribute. Omnipresence means that God is everywhere, such that no aspect of reality is apart from His presence. Saint Thomas Aquinas speaks of God's omnipresence this way:

> God is in all things by His power, inasmuch as all things are subject to His power; He is by His presence in all things, inasmuch as all things are bare and open to His eyes; He is in all things by His essence, inasmuch as He is present to all as the cause of their being.[8]

This means that God infuses and penetrates every aspect of reality. The famous "Saint Patrick's Breastplate" speaks of it this way: "Christ beside me, Christ before me, Christ behind me, Christ within me, Christ beneath me, Christ above me." While we may

---

[8] Aquinas, *Summa Theologica*, I, q.8, a.3.

apprehend His presence in varying degrees depending on the situation, this limitation is only on our part since God has no such limitation. God simply is. Thus, while we can, figuratively speaking, turn our backs on Him, He is nonetheless always present to us. To better appreciate God's presence as it relates to divine abandonment and diaconal spirituality, it will be helpful to consider the manner in which God revealed himself in the Book of Exodus.

While tending the flock of his father-in-law, Jethro, at the foot of Mount Horeb, Moses encounters an angel in the form of fire flaming out of a bush that, while burning, is not consumed. After a brief dialog with God, from which he would be sent on a mission, Moses asks:

> "If I go to the Israelites and say to them, 'The God of your ancestors has sent me to you,' and they ask me, 'What is his name?' what do I tell them?" God replied to Moses: I am who I am. Then he added: This is what you will tell the Israelites: I AM has sent me to you. (Ex 3:13–14)

In Greek and Roman mythology, when the gods came to earth, they typically did so in a violent and competitive fashion. Something in this world had to diminish or be destroyed in order for them to make themselves present. The realm of the gods and the realm of men were mutually exclusive — never the twain should meet. Consequently, in these great sagas, when men stood in the physical presence of the gods, they were often weakened or even killed. This is not the case with the God of Israel. When God draws near Moses, His presence (exhibited in the fire) does not consume the bush (which reflects us). The material and the spiritual worlds coexist side-by-side. Our God's presence does not destroy us. He doesn't compete violently with us. Instead, He illuminates us, radiating His glory in every direction. When we open ourselves up to the presence of God already within us, we become more fully alive, more perfect, more beautiful. And then we become a source of light for others.

After Moses is given his mission, he asks for God's name, to which God replies, "I am who I am." Keep in mind that Moses was raised an Egyptian prince and, after escaping Pharaoh, was living in the Sinai Peninsula among nomadic tribes. Both the Egyptians and these tribes worshiped many gods. From this perspective, Moses' question is rather commonsensical. Moses, desiring to better fulfill his mission, seeks to ground that mission in the one who sends him; he wants to distinguish this deity from all others. But God doesn't answer Moses' question, at least not directly. He simply says, "I am who I am. … Tell the Israelites: I AM has sent me to you."

Our Catholic Tradition has found this passage deeply theological, concealing as much as it reveals. In His response to Moses, God doesn't imply that He is a type of being, nor does He suggest that He is one being among many. He does not even indicate that He is the greatest being ever. Rather, he states that He is being itself. Later theologians, led by Saint Thomas Aquinas, would speak of God as *ipsum esse subsistens* ("being itself subsisting"). To be sure, this is a kind of "head-scratching" mystery for both theologians and nontheologians alike. Thankfully, for our purposes, we needn't plumb the depths of Aristotelian metaphysics. We need only observe that for Thomas and others, God does not fit in any single category of being.

To better appreciate what I mean here, consider that when we want to know about something, we tend to place it in a familiar category. If, for example, I ask, "What's that in your hands?" You might respond, "It's a book." Immediately, you have situated the unknown object in a familiar category, thus making it known, at least on a basic level. By putting things in various known categories, we can identify and differentiate them, enabling us to compare and contrast them to other things. This is the way our minds work. This is the way we come to know.

However, Aquinas asserts that God, as He has revealed himself to us, can't be put into any category, not even the category of being. He is neither "this" thing, nor "that" thing, nor even the biggest thing. He is the sheer act of being itself. If God were one thing among many, He would by necessity have to displace us, figuratively speaking, pushing us out of the way when we encounter Him. Just as I'm unable to move into your space without moving you, so it would be with a god who is simply another thing. That god, like the gods of Greek and Roman mythology, would have to violate our space and compete with us aggressively. But a God who *is* the sheer act of being can enter intimately into His creatures in a nondestructive and noncompetitive way. As the soul animates the body and gives it life, so God permeates and penetrates the lives of those who respond to His divine invitation.

Nowhere is the coexistence between the spiritual and material, between the divine and the human, expressed more profoundly than in the Incarnation. According to the *Catechism*:

> The unique and altogether singular event of the Incarnation of the Son of God does not mean that Jesus Christ is part God and part man, nor does it imply that he is the result of a confused mixture of the divine and the human. He became truly man while remaining truly God. Jesus Christ is true God and true man. (464)

The Incarnation reveals that human beings were created from the very beginning to receive the divine more perfectly than a hand receives a glove. Although sin distorts the fit in our case, grace restores it. If this is true, and we believe that it is, then does it not follow that we were made for God such that "'in him we live and move and have our being'" (Acts 17:28)?

By better grasping the nature of God and our ultimate end in Him, we can begin to see how His omnipresence means that every single moment of our lives can represent a kind of personal revelation. This revelation, in turn, can represent an opportunity for prayer. As Saint Paul of the Cross observes: "By habitually thinking of the presence of God, we succeed in praying twenty-four hours a day. The continual remembrance of the presence of God engenders in the soul a divine state." This isn't at all to suggest that God expects us to be so attentive to His revelation that we cease to live out our lives, stuck in a kind of perpetual listening and thereby neglecting our vocational responsibilities. Instead, it means that as we live out our lives — in the very midst of living out our vocations as husbands, fathers, and deacons — God's revelation is made known to us. We must take great care not to try to escape this world to find God, for if we do that, we will only succeed in passing Him on the way. He is always present, enmeshed in the very fabric of our lives.

This understanding of God is important to our consideration of abandonment because we can tend to see the spiritual life as a zero-sum game, thinking that the more I give to God, the less there is for me, my wife, my children, my ministry, and so forth. In a zero-sum game, each participant's gain or loss is proportionate to the losses or gains of the others. Perhaps an example would prove helpful. My wife and I are blessed with many children. Over the years, as the numbers grew, well-intentioned people asked, "How do you do it?" Their unspoken assumption was that the love that inspires the raising of children diminishes with each child. While it's certainly true that we humans are limited and, as a result, can be overwhelmed at times, we can, by cooperating with grace, extend those limitations. With God, we can be far more than we can be without Him. In this respect, love is not a divider but a multiplier.

By abandoning ourselves to divine providence, by slowly surrendering ourselves to the love of God, we don't lose our life. Instead, we gain it. This is precisely what Jesus meant when He spoke of discipleship: "Whoever wishes to come after me must deny himself, take up his cross, and follow me. For whoever wishes to save his life will lose it, but whoever loses his life for my sake will find it" (Mt 16:24–25). Divine abandonment means giving it all, holding nothing back, and trusting that God will provide. So with God not only is there room for our wives, our children, and our ministry, but the room for each of these grows within us. It's not that God miraculously expands the hours of the day and our energy in a quantitative sense. Rather, through our abandoning ourselves to His love, the quality of our time with each of these is enriched and enlivened. This is because God, who is present in every moment, infuses every moment with grace.

In the pursuit of divine abandonment, it's not unusual for some to slip into the extreme of providentialism. In its most basic sense, providentialism is the belief that all events are controlled by God. It's a form of fatalism that fails to see that the abandonment talked of by the saints and mystics requires an active engagement with God. We don't become a kind of puppet, responding to the strings God pulls. Rather, because He loves us, ours is a participation in His divine will in which we don't lose our own will, but instead direct it to what is true, good, and beautiful. This is analogous to a strong sacramental marriage in which the two share in one life, albeit as two distinct individuals. Thus, my will is shaped and influenced by my wife's will, while always remaining my own. Because it remains my will, the acts that flow from it are my acts; the love that I give is my love.

THE SACRAMENT OF THE PRESENT MOMENT

The events of every moment bear the impress of the
will of God, and of His adorable Name. How holy is
this name! It's right, therefore, to bless it, to treat it as
a kind of sacrament which by its own virtue sanctifies
those souls which place no obstacles in its way.
Jean-Pierre de Caussade,
Abandonment to Divine Providence

Thus far we've examined the primacy of the interior life, the distinctiveness of diaconal spirituality, and divine abandonment as these relate to the ever-present God. To appreciate these foundational points as they pertain to the life and ministry of the deacon, we now turn to what de Caussade calls "the sacrament of the present moment" or, more often, "the present moment." The sacrament of the present moment is the realization that the ever-present God makes himself known to us through everyday events such as the people we meet, the places we go, and even our struggles. Of this de Caussade writes, "God continues to speak today as He spoke in former times to our fathers when there were no [spiritual] directors as at present, nor any regular method of direction."[9]

The "speech of God" is a figurative way of describing how God communicates with us. This is also known as Divine Revelation. By Divine Revelation, the Church means God's self-disclosure of who He is and His plan for our salvation. There are three kinds of revelation, the most important of which is public. The Fathers of the Second Vatican Council, in *Dei Verbum* (Dogmatic Constitution on Divine Revelation), described public Revelation this way:

---

[9] De Caussade, *Abandonment*, 6.

After God had spoken many times and in various ways through the prophets, "in these last days He has spoken to us by a Son" (Heb. 1:1–2). For he sent his Son, the eternal Word who enlightens all men, to dwell among men and to tell them about the inner life of God. Hence, Jesus Christ, sent as "a man among men" ... accomplishes the saving work which the Father gave Him to do (cf. Jn. 5:36; 17:4). As a result, he himself ... completed and perfected Revelation and confirmed it with divine guarantees. ... No new public revelation is to be expected before the glorious manifestation of our Lord Jesus Christ.[10]

Public Revelation, found in Scripture and Tradition, constitutes the Sacred Deposit of Faith, that which all believers are called to believe. While it's complete in the sense that mankind has received all that is needed for salvation, "it has not been made completely explicit; it remains for Christian faith gradually to grasp its significance over the course of the centuries" (CCC 66). As the authentic guardians of the Faith, the Magisterium or teaching office of the Church — that is, the bishops in union with the pope — under the guidance of the Holy Spirit, interpret this Revelation, keeping it free from error. Because of this, the faithful, precisely because they have chosen to be faithful, are to accept these revealed truths with a divine faith. Explicitly rejecting truths such as the Incarnation, the Real Presence, or even the existence of Satan would constitute an infidelity.

Unlike public Revelation, which ended with the death of the last apostle, private revelation is meant to emphasize that which has already been revealed. It's a divine message, given through a certain person or persons, that helps the faithful to grow in holiness. According to the *Catechism*, "Throughout the ages, there

---

[10] *Dei Verbum*, 4.

have been so-called 'private' revelations, some of which have been recognized by the authority of the Church. ... It is not their role to improve or complete Christ's definitive Revelation, but to help live more fully by it" (67). Those who have received private revelations include many saints, including Saint Catherine of Siena, Saint Teresa of Ávila, Saint John of the Cross, Saint Margaret Mary Alacoque, and Saint Faustina Kowalska, to name a few. Private revelation also includes the various apparitions of the Blessed Virgin Mary as she speaks on behalf of her Son. Some of the better-known Marian apparitions have been Our Lady of Guadalupe, Our Lady of the Miraculous Medal at the chapel at Rue du Bac, Our Lady of La Salette, Our Lady of Lourdes, and Our Lady of Fátima. The authenticity of any private revelation, be it purportedly from Jesus, from a saint, or from the Blessed Mother, lies in its agreement with public Revelation. Although the Church may officially recognize and approve the content of these private revelations, they neither belong to nor add anything to the Sacred Deposit of Faith. They simply emphasize that which has already been revealed, inspiring the faithful to grow in deeper communion with God. For this reason, the faithful are not required to accept private revelation. That said, it would be imprudent for anyone wishing to grow in holiness not to at least investigate the implications of private revelation for the interior life.

Personal revelation is another kind of revelation, which God gives to an individual to discern His will in a particular situation. Like private revelation, personal revelation must be in agreement with public Revelation and the teachings of the Church in order to be considered authentic. It may arise in such situations as discerning a vocation, a new job, a move, or even a major expense. Our understanding of personal revelation is based on two fundamental truths. The first is that God loves us and cares about every detail of our lives. Because of this, He provides to all who are open to them the interior insights necessary to live the Christian life. For our purposes as deacons, this would include a deep and constant revelation of Christ the Servant as He relates to our identity and mission. The second fundamental truth is that God wants us to use our reason and free will to do good and avoid evil. Where the first truth concerns the interior life, the second pertains to the exterior life.

The sacrament of the present moment represents a kind of personal revelation that is constant and ongoing. Unlike other kinds of personal revelation, it doesn't concern itself with something specific such as a vocation, job, or house but instead focuses on an ongoing awareness of God's presence in the here and now. As de Caussade points out, "What treasures of grace lie concealed in these moments filled, apparently, by the most ordinary events. That which is visible might happen to anyone, but the invisible, discerned by faith, is no less than God operating very great things."[11] If we have eyes to see, the present moment provides divine encounters that reveal something of God.

De Caussade treats this personal revelation broadly, such that every moment reveals the majesty of God. For our purposes, we will assume this approach and build upon it, advancing de Caussade's thought by considering its application to the diaconate. Here, our concern is how the sacrament of the present moment allows the deacon to see the suffering Christ in the needs of others and to minister to those needs effectively. Before we begin, however, some important distinctions are in order.

Because of his ordination to the diaconate, the deacon has been configured on the deepest level of his being to Christ the Servant. As such, he is the sacred custodian of ecclesial service, bearing witness to Christ the Servant by "incarnating" Him in the life of the Church. In this respect, he is called, as revealed in the groundbreaking work of John N. Collins, to be an am-

---

[11] De Caussade, *Abandonment*, 7.

bassador or emissary.[12] This understanding of the diaconate will be taken up in greater detail in the next chapter; for now, it points out the deacon's particular role in the mystery of salvation and the life of the Church. It is this role, arising from his diaconal ordination, that reorients the deacon as he approaches the sacrament of the present moment. Consequently, the deacon, while attentive to all that God wants to reveal to him, must be particularly attentive to the needs of others and to how these needs might be fulfilled. For the servant, in this case the deacon, to serve the master, he must know what the master needs and when he needs it. Simply put, the servant must love the master through specific concrete acts. This side of heaven, we can't love God directly any more than we can serve Him directly. We can, however, love and serve Him through loving and serving others. Recall the words of Jesus in Matthew's Gospel: "Amen, I say to you, whatever you did for one of these least brothers of mine, you did for me" (Mt 25:40).

When de Caussade wrote to the sisters in the eighteenth century, the term "duty" was understood within the spiritual tradition as an obligation arising out of a divine love already bestowed — as a concrete application of the virtue of religion, which itself is an expression of the cardinal virtue of justice. In the work of de Caussade, "duty" is understood as rendering God His due. Of course, in reality, it is impossible to render to God what is due to Him since the love we've received from Him far exceeds our ability to respond in kind. It's only when our response, meager though it is, is united with Christ's own love and offered back to the Father that our duty has been fulfilled. It is Christ, and Christ alone, who makes up our deficit and, in doing so, bridges the gap between what was given and what is returned, thereby

---

[12] In this work, the terms "envoy," "emissary," "ambassador," and "intermediary" are used synonymously. All convey, with slightly different nuances, one entrusted with a great mission who bears the authority of the one who sent him.

satisfying our duty. This isn't a one-time event but, because God continues to pour out His love upon us, a constant and ongoing reality, a kind of reciprocity that never ends unless we end it. De Caussade describes duty this way:

> For those who led a spiritual life, each moment brought some duty to be faithfully accomplished. Their whole attention was thus concentrated consecutively like a hand that marks the hours which, at each moment, traverses the space allotted to it. Their minds, incessantly animated by the impulsion of divine grace, turned imperceptibly to each new duty that presented itself by the permission of God at different hours of the day.[13]

Because in contemporary thought "duty" implies a burdensome responsibility, often unfairly imposed, placing de Caussade's use of the term within the context of divine love provides a necessary corrective. It also demonstrates the importance of the sacrament of the present moment as it pertains to diaconal ministry. If, in the present moment, we perceive the suffering Christ in others, then our duty arising from that perception is an act of love, and that act of love is nothing less than authentic diaconal ministry. Without the sacrament of the present moment, without recognizing Christ throughout our day, we pass right by Him. He goes unseen in our hearts, unnoticed in our ministry, and ultimately unappreciated in our lives. For the deacon, sensitivity to the sacrament of the present moment is made possible through an ongoing encounter with the Servant Mysteries.

---

[13] De Caussade, *Abandonment*, 6.

Chapter Three
The Servant Mysteries

*O my Lord, inflame my heart with love for
You, that my spirit may not grow weary amidst
the storms, the sufferings and the trials. You
see how weak I am. Love can do all.*
**Saint Maria Faustina Kowalska, *Diary of Saint Maria
Faustina Kowalska: Divine Mercy in My Soul***

As noted earlier, the Servant Mysteries are the revelation of Christ the Servant as made known in the sacrament of the present moment. They are everyday encounters found in prayer and ministry, in work and play, and indeed in all aspects of life, disclosing to the deacon the true meaning of authentic Christian servanthood. These mysteries are most fully revealed in the Passion, Death, and Resurrection of Jesus Christ. Far more than a specific kind of sacred knowledge, these mysteries offer insight into the person and mission of Jesus Christ, inviting the deacon into a more intimate communion with Him. In this respect, the Servant Mysteries are fundamentally relational. They enable the deacon, as he draws closer to his Master, to grow in his diaconate, bearing witness to Christ the Servant in a preeminent and exemplary way.

According to the *Basic Norms for the Formation of Permanent Deacons*, "The element which most characterizes diaconal spirituality is the discovery of and sharing in the love of Christ the Servant, who came not to be served but to serve."[1] When a deacon actively engages in divine abandonment, the Servant Mysteries are revealed in the sacrament of the present moment, and in these moments, the deacon encounters Christ the Servant. These encounters, in turn, capacitate the deacon to mystically identify with Him, to fall in love with Him, to be transformed by Him, and then, and only then, to serve Him. This is why to characterize these mysteries as simply "places" in Scripture and Tradition where Christ's servanthood is revealed misses something far more profound — the very purpose of that Revelation.

A BEAUTY THAT WOUNDS

> *It will happen that while the soul is inflamed with the Love of God, it will feel that a seraph is assailing it by means of an arrow or dart which is all afire with love. And the seraph pierces and in an instant cauterizes [burns] this soul, which, like a red-hot coal, or better a flame, is already enkindled. The soul is converted into an immense fire of Love.*
> **Saint John of the Cross on the Transverberation of Saint Teresa of Ávila's Heart**

---

[1] Congregation for Catholic Education and Congregation for the Clergy, *Basic Norms for the Formation of Permanent Deacons* (Vatican City: Libreria Editrice Vaticana, 1998), 72.

In his book *The Heart of the Diaconate*, Deacon James Keating speaks of the Servant Mysteries as Christ's own heart being "pressed" into the heart of the deacon at ordination.[2] This "impression" is an intense encounter that forever changes him. In what at first seems rather strange language, Keating speaks of ordination as a kind of deep wounding. In this wounding, the deacon's heart is lacerated by Christ's own beauty and the beauty of His mission. This way of speaking makes sense only when ordination, and indeed the whole of the diaconate, is understood within the context of a deep, intimate communion with Christ the Servant. Saint John of the Cross tenderly expresses this intimacy when he writes, "For when the flame of divine life wounds the soul with the gentle languishing for the life of God, it wounds it with so much tenderness, and softens it so that it melts away in love."[3]

The analogy of marriage is helpful in explaining this notion of woundedness. In marriage, a husband, deeply in love with his wife, is wounded by her inner beauty. He sees in her something so precious that he is driven to his knees, injured, so to speak, by her profound loveliness. Popular romantic terms such as "longing," "pining", and "yearning" all bespeak the kind of suffering that comes from a woundedness inflicted by this beauty. A similar illustration occurs on Saint Valentine's Day, with a heart pierced by an arrow. Here, it's important to recognize that this kind of beauty isn't mere physical allure, but something much deeper. It concerns the attractiveness of her entire being such that her being makes up what is missing in the husband. She fulfills an emptiness, and her presence brings a kind of fulfillment and satisfaction. Consequently, what he desires isn't something about her, some desirable trait, but simply the wife herself. The

---

[2] Keating, *Heart of the Diaconate*, 61–62; see also James Keating, "Identity and Holiness," in *The Character of the Deacon*, ed. James Keating (New York/Mahwah, NJ: Paulist Press, 2017), 127–28.
[3] John of the Cross, *The Living Flame of Love* (New York: Cosmo Classics, 2007), 9.

perception of this inner beauty enables him to glimpse, ever so slightly, what God sees in her; and that inner beauty far exceeds any physical quality she may have, no matter how sensually attractive that quality may be. This is why, as his wife grows older, she becomes even more beautiful to him, despite the effects of age. Reflecting on this kind of beauty and the woundedness it brings, Cardinal Joseph Ratzinger (now Pope Emeritus Benedict XVI), writes:

> For Plato, beauty in fact is a cause of suffering. The encounter with it comes as a shock which takes the individual out of his everyday existence and nurtures in him a longing for the original perfection that was conceived for him and which he has since lost. The shock of the encounter with beauty is like an arrow that pierces man, wounds him and in this way gives him wings, lifts him upwards toward the transcendent. … The longing elicited by beauty finds its healing, through the revelation of the New Testament, in the Truth which redeems. … When men have a longing so great that it passes human nature … it's the Bridegroom himself who has wounded them. Into their eyes he himself has sent a ray of beauty.[4]

In the diaconate, the deacon is wounded by Christ's inner beauty, particularly as that beauty is revealed in the Servant Mysteries through the sacrament of the present moment. The deacon sees in these mysteries a Servant so precious that he is driven to his knees, injured, so to speak, by the outpouring of this Servant's love for humanity and for him. This is precisely what Saint Augustine meant when he observed, "In my deepest wound I saw

---

your glory and it dazzled me."[5] As the deacon allows Christ to draw close, particularly through the Servant Mysteries, His Divine Presence reveals an emptiness within the deacon, a place that Christ the Servant, and only Christ the Servant, can fill. So, prior to ordination and even after, he longs, pines, and yearns for this fulfillment — and this bespeaks the kind of suffering that comes from a woundedness inflicted by Christ's beauty. Because this fulfillment won't reach its perfection until he stands before the throne of God and is judged worthy, this woundedness and the suffering that accompanies it will last throughout his diaconate, bringing with it a fulfillment that's never quite fulfilled, a satisfaction that's never quite satisfied.

Here, what attracts isn't something *about* Christ — it's not simply some aspect of His life, Passion, Death, and Resurrection — but instead something much deeper. It concerns the attractiveness of His entire being, such that His being makes up what is missing in the deacon. Christ the Servant fulfills an emptiness, and His Divine Presence brings a kind of consolation that overcomes any desolation. Consequently, what is desired isn't something about Christ, some desirable trait, some aspect of His ministry, but simply Christ himself. The perception of this inner beauty enables the deacon to glimpse, ever so slightly, God; and that inner beauty far exceeds any aspect of Christ's life, no matter how profound that aspect may be. This is why, as the deacon progresses over the years in his diaconate, Christ the Servant becomes even more beautiful to him, despite the routineness and frustrations often associated with pastoral ministry.

Ordinarily, we think of wounding as something negative, and it certainly can be. This negative kind of wounding is characterized by a malicious intent, often accompanied by physical or emotional violence. Here, the one being wounded is treated as an object to be used, possessed, and discarded at the end of the day.

---

[5] Augustine, *Confessions*, ed. William Mann (Oxford: Oxford University Press, 2014), 67.

This negative wounding is antithetical to the positive wounding found in such relationships as marriage. Positive wounding is characterized by a beneficial intent accompanied by a deep consideration for the other. Here, the one being wounded, in this case the husband, is treated by the one wounding, his wife, not as an object to be used but rather as a person to be loved, respected, and valued. In this case, the husband, so moved by the beauty of the wife, doesn't desire to possess her as in negative wounding, but instead desires to be possessed by her. In this dynamic, love moves between the husband and wife in a mutual way such that both allow themselves to be wounded by the other.

Likewise, the positive wounding received in ordination and lived throughout a deacon's life, is characterized by a beneficial intent accompanied by a deep consideration for the other. Here, the one being wounded, in this case the deacon, is treated by the one wounding, Christ, not as an object to be used but rather as a person to be respected and valued. The deacon, so moved by the beauty of Christ the Servant, doesn't desire to possess Him, but instead desires to be possessed by Him. In this dynamic, love moves between the deacon and Christ in a mutual way such that both allow themselves to be wounded by the other.

For wounding to take place on the level of marriage, the beauty that attracts must be *unique and proper to the couple*. This happens when both recognize a calling, a vocation, to marry each other. The world is chock full of people who possess inner beauty and, while all of them are attractive in some way, each can choose only one to share in the mutual woundedness that is marriage. In this case, woundedness is exclusive to one. Only one can be permitted to wound me, and certitude that this is the one comes when she desires to be wounded *by me*. In this respect, there's always a double wounding.

The same is true with the diaconate. When discerning, the candidate may want to be wounded by ordination, but if the formators representing the local bishop don't recognize in the candidate the particular kind of beauty proper to the diaconate, then the discernment process can't move forward. Ordination represents not simply a wounding of the one being ordained but the willingness of the Church and, by extension, Christ the Servant to be wounded by him. Christ already bears these wounds for the deacon through the Paschal Mystery. His Passion, Death, and Resurrection, being timeless and eternal, are diaconally applied to the newly ordained.

As the deacon seeks to live out the Servant Mysteries, the beauty that wounds arises first in his ordination and then in his imitation of Christ the Servant. His redemptive love, expressed in service, always wounds, and the suffering from these wounds characterizes Jesus as the Suffering Servant. Suffering, in this respect, flows from a woundedness, and woundedness flows from the profound beauty that Christ recognizes in His Bride the Church. It was this beauty that motivated Him to take up His Cross, be wounded in His Passion, and suffer death. This suffering, then, marks the quality of sacred service, affirming its authenticity with respect to Christ.

What gives this suffering its excellence and nobility isn't the pain and hardship it brings but, as in the case of Christ's suffering, the application of this pain and heartache to the salvation it offers. This is the only suitable response to the woundedness experienced because it is the only response capable of expressing the love felt. Beauty, woundedness, and suffering — as these relate to the deacon and his ministry — draw him and those he serves into deep, intimate communion with Christ. They participate, each in their own way, in the salvific mission of Christ, who continues to extend His hands into the world through the ministry of the deacon. Because he shares in a unique way in Christ's own servanthood, the deacon, wounded by Christ, now shares in His suffering. He becomes a suffering servant like his Master.

The quality of suffering as it relates to sacred ecclesial service, revealed by Christ and witnessed by the diaconate, was foreshadowed by the prophet Isaiah. In four distinct but related songs, we learn that God will choose a servant to bring justice to the world, not by political or military action but by working quietly and confidently to establish right religion. He will restore Israel, but not without cost and not without being wounded:

> He was spurned and avoided by men,
> > a man of suffering, knowing pain,
> Like one from whom you turn your face,
> > spurned, and we held him in no esteem.
>
> Yet it was our pain that he bore,
> > our sufferings he endured.
> We thought of him as stricken,
> > struck down by God and afflicted,
> But he was pierced for our sins,
> > crushed for our iniquity.
> He bore the punishment that makes us whole,
> > by his wounds we were healed. ...
>
> My servant, the just one, shall justify the many. (Isaiah 53:3–5, 11)

The Scriptures directly identify Isaiah's Suffering Servant as Jesus. In the Acts of the Apostles, Saint Luke describes a meeting between the deacon Philip and an Ethiopian eunuch on the road from Jerusalem to Gaza. There, Philip asks, "Do you understand what you are reading?" to which the Ethiopian responds, "How can I, unless someone instructs me?" At that point, "Philip opened his mouth and, beginning with this scripture passage, he proclaimed Jesus to him" (see Acts 8:26–35). The Church has long seen Jesus as the Suffering Servant, so much so that the early Church Fathers dubbed the Suffering Servant Songs as the "Fifth Gospel."

It's fascinating to observe that the first one to recognize and apply Isaiah's Suffering Servant to Christ is a deacon. One could speculate that insofar as Philip was called to live out the Servant Mysteries, he recognized in the experience of Christ's own suffering a quality of service, an expression of divine love. Perhaps this quality resonated so profoundly within Philip's heart, it having been wounded by Christ the Servant in his own call to *diakonia,* that he could reach no other conclusion when the Ethiopian eunuch asked, "I beg you, about whom is the prophet saying this?" (Acts 8:34). To this, "Philip opened his mouth and, beginning with this scripture passage, he proclaimed Jesus to him" (Acts 8:35).

KEEPING OPEN THE WOUNDS

> *I do not desire to die soon, because in Heaven there is no suffering. I desire to live a long time because I yearn to suffer much for the love of my Spouse.*
> **Saint Mary Magdalene de Pazzi,** *Letters*

Just as Christ's wounds remain open so that future generations may experience beyond His own time the saving effect of that woundedness, the deacon must, as Deacon Keating often points out, keep his wounds fresh so that he can effectively fulfill his mission.[6] In this respect, the woundedness that arises out of ordination is akin to internal stigmata. As the stigmata are outward signs of a participation in Christ's own woundedness and a sharing of His salvific mission, diaconal wounding finds it source and strength in Christ the Servant.

Saint Francis of Assisi, a deacon himself, bore the stigma-

---

[6] Keating, *Heart of the Diaconate*, 62.

ta; in doing so, he manifested in his body what he was already suffering in his soul. Two years prior to his death, while Francis was in deep prayer on a remote mountaintop in La Verna, Italy, an angel representing Christ mounted on a cross appeared to him. At the request of Pope Gregory IX, Thomas of Celano later wrote an account of this event based on the testimony of the two friars who accompanied Francis. In it, he conveys:

> The marks of nails began to appear in his hands and feet, just as he had seen them slightly earlier in the crucified man above him. His wrists and feet seemed to be pierced by nails, with the heads of the nails appearing on his wrists and on the upper sides of his feet, the points appearing on the other side. … In the same way the marks of nails were impressed on his feet and projected beyond the rest of the flesh. Moreover, his right side had a large wound as if it had been pierced with a spear.[7]

Once received, these wounds remained open for the rest of Francis's life. They reflected a life lived in intense communion with Christ the Servant, such that Jesus' sufferings became Francis's sufferings. Although few are called to experience this kind of heroic virtue on the outside, all deacons are called and graced to live it on the inside. Christ the Servant is revealed in the deacon's life and ministry to the extent that the deacon is open to acknowledging the interior stigmata received at ordination and to the extent that he seeks to live this wounding out in the sacrament of the present moment. While such a call carries with it all of the sufferings associated with the wounds, it is not without its consolations. Of Francis's wounds Saint Bonaventure

---

[7] Thomas of Celano, *The First Life of St. Francis of Assisi*, trans. Christopher Stace (London:, Society for Promoting Christian Knowledge, 2000), 96.

later wrote, "The sight of it amazed Francis and his soul experienced joy mingled with pain. He was delighted with the sight of Christ appearing to him so graciously and intimately and … [it] aroused in his soul a joy of compassionate love."[8]

Following the example of Saint Francis, deacons keep open the wound of ordination primarily through a participation in the Servant Mysteries as they are revealed, first and foremost, in the interior life. Here, through deep prayer, meditation, and even contemplation, we encounter Christ the Servant, whose beauty surpasses that of all others. When we seek this encounter genuinely sought in a state of grace, Jesus reaches out and touches us, and we, so moved by His beauty, are wounded. This woundedness arises out of an experience of being loved well beyond what we believe our worth to be and being sent on a mission that far exceeds our natural capacities. Echoing the words of King David before God, we say, "Who am I, Lord GOD, and what is my house, that you should have brought me so far?" (2 Sm 7:18).

This outpouring of divine love through multiple encounters with Christ the Servant in the Servant Mysteries keeps open the wounds. This woundedness then bleeds over into our life and ministry, bringing with it a humility proper to being a good and faithful servant. Returning again and again to the Servant Mysteries, the font of the deacon's diaconate, we keep fresh this precious wound that enables us to suffer for Christ and, perhaps more to the point, to suffer well. Here, the prayer of diaconal ordination, the prayer that originally wounded us, is particularly helpful as we seek to relive and live out the gift of our diaconate.

This gift, because it wounds, renders the deacon "permanently available," in Keating's words, to receive these very same mysteries throughout his life.[9] Because the Servant Mysteries

---

[8] Bonaventure, *The Minor Legend*, chap. 6, 2nd lesson, accessed January 2020, https://www.franciscantradition.org/francis-of-assisi-early-documents/the-founder/the-legends-and-sermons-about-saint-francis-by-bonaventure-of-bagnoregio/the-minor-legend/1798-fa-ed-2-page-709.

[9] Keating, *Heart of the Diaconate*, 14, 63.

represent the deacon's ongoing encounters with Christ the Servant, they represent the very soul of the diaconate. Just as our soul infuses the body, giving it life, the soul of the diaconate — the Servant Mysteries — infuses the deacon's ministry with new life. As Keating observes, when the deacon is faithful to these mysteries, he becomes the living embodiment of them, rendering him radically capable of bearing witness to Christ the Servant. As a result, he is the custodian of sacred ecclesial service. Because of this, his life and ministry ought to inspire laity and clergy alike to embrace these very same Servant Mysteries proper to their respective vocations. As the *Basic Norms for the Formation of Permanent Deacons* observes:

> The spirituality of service is a spirituality of the whole Church, insofar as the whole Church, in the same way as Mary, is the "handmaid of the Lord" (Lk 1:28), at the service of the salvation of the world. And so that the whole Church may better live out this spirituality of service, the Lord gives her a living and personal sign of his very being as servant. In a specific way, this is the spirituality of the deacon. In fact, with sacred ordination, he is constituted a living icon of Christ the servant within the Church.[10]

Our discussion thus far points out the essential nature of the Servant Mysteries in the life of the deacon. Assumed in all of this is a common understanding of the terms that make up the phrase "Servant Mysteries." If "servant" and "mysteries" are grasped in a popular sense, without exploring their theological nuances, more is missed than gained. As a result, we would do well to reflect upon these terms in an attempt to shed greater insight on the Revelation that is Christ the Servant.

---

[10] *Basic Norms*, 4.

The Greek term *diákonos*, commonly rendered as "servant" or "minister," was probably derived from the obsolete verb *diōkō*, meaning "to run errands." Though rare in Classical Greek and uncommon in the Septuagint, different forms of the *diakon*-word group appear over a hundred times in the New Testament. In his contribution to Kittel's *Theological Dictionary of the New Testament*, the German scholar Hermann W. Beyer holds that the verb *diakoneō* means simply "to serve" or "to provide and care for." Beyer was highly influenced by the thesis of Wilhelm Brandt, who in turn was influenced by the Lutheran Deaconess Movement of the late nineteenth century. By this time, the German term *Diakonie*, taken from the Greek, had come to designate Christian social work. It was from this ministerial association that Beyer saw a strong link to Christian service. This understanding was picked up and circulated among many of the lesser-known lexicons and commentaries of the time. Since many Catholic scholars used these Protestant sources after the restoration of the diaconate by the Second Vatican Council and since these sources were far more concerned with ministry than with scriptural or patristic usage, the Catholic understanding followed the Protestant concept of *diákonos* as one who serves the poor and needy.

This rather widespread notion of *diakonia* as service was challenged in 1990 by the Australian linguist John N. Collins. In his groundbreaking book *Diakonia: Re-Interpreting the Ancient Sources*, Collins focuses on the nature and function of Christian ministry.[11] He conducts an exhaustive study of the term *diakonia* using both Christian and non-Christian sources from about 200 B.C. to A.D. 200. Collins concludes that in all of these sources, the term means an envoy, an emissary, or a messenger and has little to do with care for the poor and needy as such. Instead, he

---

[11] John N. Collins, *Diakonia: Re-Interpreting Ancient Sources* (New York: Oxford University Press, 1990).

maintains that Jesus' *diakonia* is done out of compassion and love for others *as an envoy of the Father*.[12]

Collins brilliantly puts the emphasis of Christian service back where it belongs, shifting the object of *diakonia* away from the thing being done to a concrete expression of divine love. A minister of service is not simply a doer of good things but an envoy of God's love in the service of which good things are done. The deacon's service is first and foremost to God rather than to the people; only in God and with His grace can he truly serve the people. Understood this way, Collins's contribution moves Christian service away from a purely functional work to a deeply relational encounter. Here, the deacon is called to stand in between God and the people as a divine ambassador and proclaim the Gospel, which is precisely what he does in the liturgy. Collins's breakthrough undercuts much of the theological discussion on the diaconate that has taken place since its restoration by the Fathers of the Second Vatican Council.

By reenvisioning *diakonia* and reanchoring it in the language of the Early Church as an envoy or a messenger of divine love, Collins implicitly presupposes an intimate relationship of trust and responsibility between the servant and God. This is why the cultivation of the interior life is essential to living out our diaconate: It provides the "interior place" to know and love the One who sends us. It's precisely this love of God that becomes the primary motivation for the deacon's diaconate. It sources his strength in the One who sends him, thereby enriching his ministry with a distinctively divine quality. Without this essential quality, the deacon becomes a mere social worker; and while there is nothing wrong with social work, it's not his calling.

Collins's research influenced the scholarly community so much that it is responsible for redefining the entry on the *diakon-* word group in *A Greek Lexicon of the New Testament and*

---

[12] Ibid., 195–215.

Early Christian Literature. This was no easy task, as many of these definitions have long been ensconced in the annals of linguistic dogma. I came to the same conclusion as Collins while research-ing and writing *In the Person of Christ the Servant*, albeit from a different starting point. As I carefully read the story of the estab-lishment of the diaconate in Acts 6, then the narratives associated with Stephen and Philip, along with the place of the diaconate in the early Church, it was pretty apparent to me that "service at ta-ble" isn't meant to be taken literally.[13]

Applying the personalist thought of Pope Saint John Paul II, we see that the deacon exercises his diaconate by bringing forth divine love through a salvific gift-of-self that wills the good (happiness) of the other for the sake of the other.[14] Be-cause he can't give what he hasn't first received, this diaconal gift has its source in a prior gift, the gift to the deacon of Christ's own *diakonia* at his ordination. It is in deep gratitude for and profound appreciation of this gift that the deacon is empow-ered and commissioned to be the emissary he is. This empow-erment and commissioning, begun at ordination, sacramental-ly bonds his identity to his mission, such that his identity now becomes his mission. There exists within him an ever-growing sense of integrity so that he does not merely exercise his min-istry; rather, he lives it in all aspects of his life, bearing living witness to the very Gospel he proclaims. As Pope Benedict XVI astutely observes:

> St. Stephen is a model for all those who want to serve the New Evangelization. He shows that the novelty of proc-lamation does not primarily consist in the use of orig-inal methods or techniques, which certainly have their uses, but in being filled with the Holy Spirit and allowing

---

[13] Cerrato, *In the Person*, 190–208.
[14] Ibid., 211.

ourselves to be guided by him. The novelty of proclamation lies in immersing ourselves deeply in the mystery of Christ, the assimilation of his word and of his presence in the Eucharist, so that he himself, the living Jesus, can act and speak *through his envoy*. (emphasis mine)[15]

Bishop W. Shawn McKnight has recently taken up the deacon as emissary in his book *Understanding the Diaconate*. Like Collins, McKnight sees the deacon as a herald who bears another's word, another's mandate. More specifically, the deacon is an envoy of his bishop. Where Collins takes a linguistic approach and delves into history, McKnight grounds his approach in theological, patristic, and liturgical sources. He writes, "The modern world cries out for the presence and the ministry of the deacon as a symbol of *communitas* and as an intermediary between the people of God and the poor. But we should not neglect the final aspect, intermediary between the people of God, including the poor, and the bishop."[16] McKnight seizes on this way of thinking to describe new and creative ministries that enable deacons to more effectively extend the love of Christ the Servant in the modern world.[17] The contributions of Collins and McKnight rescue the diaconate from the restrictive narrow definitions of the past, opening up to the deacon new possibilities of being an ambassador of divine love.

Having considered the word "servant," we now turn to its companion term in the phrase "Servant Mysteries." The word "mystery" is quite instructive. It's derived from the Greek word *mystērion*, which is also translated into the Latin word *sacramentum,* from which we get the English term "sacrament." A mys-

---

[15] Benedict XVI, Angelus (December 26, 2012, feast of Saint Stephen), accessed June 20, 2020, Vatican.va.

[16] W. Shawn McKnight, *Understanding the Diaconate* (Washington, DC: Catholic University of America Press, 2018), 270.

[17] Ibid., 235–52.

tery, in the theological sense, is that which is hidden, though not completely. It's a truth that we can't discover apart from Divine Revelation and that, even after this Revelation, far exceeds our comprehension. The prime example of a mystery is the Blessed Trinity. It's a truth that human reason can't grasp on its own and that awaits divine disclosure of its fuller meaning.

To be sure, we know that there is one God in three distinct Persons, all sharing a divine nature. We know that they are a communion of Persons, and that they are an eternal exchange of love. We know that they are called Father, Son, and Holy Spirit. That said, despite the Revelation of Jesus Christ, despite 2,000 years of Tradition guided by the Holy Spirit, we know little more. The Triune God is a mystery, one that awaits a greater Revelation. In this respect, what has been revealed particularly in Christ acts as a kind of sacrament of that which has yet to be revealed; it's a visible sign that points beyond itself to a deeper invisible reality, somehow participating in and making present the very reality to which it points.

While the Servant Mysteries admit of certain sacramental qualities, they aren't sacraments in the strict sense.[18] Nor are they mere sacramentals.[19] They fall somewhere in between, though they are more closely related to the sacraments because they flow from the diaconate, which itself is at the lower level of the Sacrament of Holy Orders. Like the sacraments themselves, the Servant Mysteries are efficacious in that it's Christ Jesus who is at work in them. It is He who acts in and through His deacons in order to communicate the grace that diaconal ministry signifies.[20] In this respect, the Servant Mysteries are outwardly perceptible signs that objectively make visible, *ex opere operato*, Christ the Servant, who himself is invisible. In the deacon and

---

[18] *Catechism of the Catholic Church*, 1131.
[19] Ibid., 1667.
[20] Ibid., 1127.

in his life, they signify and make present the graces proper to the diaconate, thereby contributing uniquely to the mystery of salvation.

As the Dominican theologian Edward Schillebeeckx points out, Jesus is the Primordial Sacrament who makes visible the invisible God, being in himself the perfect Revelation of that self-same God (see Heb 1:1–2). He is, so to speak, the very "place" of encounter with the divine. At the same time, the God that Jesus reveals still remains very much hidden. Nonetheless, what is revealed is so deeply beautiful that it wounds. The Seven Sacraments flow from and find their meaning in Christ the Primordial Sacrament, with the Church playing an essential mediating role by divine design. It's within this sacramental economy that the diaconate finds its place. Because the diaconate participates in Holy Orders, it must look to Christ for its source, meaning, and purpose.

Just as each sacrament, in its own way, makes present the Primordial Sacrament, the diaconate makes present Christ the Servant in and through the Servant Mysteries. In this sense, the Servant Mysteries are not something, but a sacred encounter with Someone, Christ the Servant, who reveals divine love through sacrificial service to His Bride, the Church. This is precisely what Christ means when He says, "Just so, the Son of Man did not come to be served but to serve and to give his life as a ransom for many" (Mt 20:28). In this respect, Jesus is the Primordial Deacon from whom all deacons find their source, meaning, and purpose. Because it's impossible to have direct contact with Him on earth, He is made sacramentally present in many ways, one of which is through the Servant Mysteries. They are sacraments in the sense of mediating divine love in a particular and unique way, and because of this, they represent an essential part of God's plan to draw humanity to himself.

To claim that it's impossible to have direct contact with God on earth is simply to say that earth is not heaven. No matter how intense our experience of God this side of eternity, it pales in comparison to what our experience will be like when we see Him face to face. This is not at all to diminish what can be called "privileged moments" during our lives. We may experience Our Lord intensely in contemplative prayer, at Eucharistic adoration, during the reception of the sacraments, or even at the birth of a child. Mystics such as Saint Juliana of Liège, Saint Catherine of Siena, Saint Teresa of Ávila, and Saint Pio of Pietrelcina all reported visions of Jesus. As authentic as these earthly visions are, they are just that — earthly visions. An earthly experience, no matter how powerful, cannot compare to the reality that awaits us should we be judged worthy and enter into the heavenly presence of God. Direct contact is what Tradition calls beatitude. According to the *Catechism of the Catholic Church*, "With beatitude, man enters into the glory of Christ and into the joy of the Trinitarian life" (1721). Every other kind of earthly contact with the Divine is indirect inasmuch as it is mediated. Just as there is a difference between an interpersonal encounter where the two parties are physically present to each other and an interpersonal encounter over a video conference call, so too there is a difference between direct contact with God and indirect contact. To be sure, much can be related over a video conference, but never quite as much as can be related in person.

As noted earlier, the Servant Mysteries are the revelation of Christ the Servant as made known in the sacrament of the present moment. As such, they play a critical role in diaconal spirituality because they allow the deacon to encounter Christ the Servant in a constant and ongoing way, thereby keeping open the wounds he received at ordination. By meditating on these mysteries, particularly in his prayer and life, the deacon comes to realize a profound truth: that the Servant Mysteries don't simply mediate authentic servanthood. As we've already observed, they mediate Someone.

Jesus Christ, the Son of the Living God, is the Primordial Servant Mystery. Reflecting on these mysteries makes Him present in a profound way to the deacon: Christ the Servant becomes more real, His presence more intense, His grace more palpable. These encounters transform the deacon from the inside out such that he now becomes the living embodiment of the Servant Mysteries. This renders him radically capable of incarnating Christ the Servant, not just in the exercise of his ministry but in every aspect of his life. In this respect, the deacon himself is a servant mystery to others, and even to himself.

INTERNALIZING THE SERVANT MYSTERIES

These mysteries, truly Christ's own heart, define the deacon's ecclesial and spiritual life. Christ opens his heart to press its servant mysteries into the heart of the deacon, imbuing the man with a defining sacramental character.
Deacon James Keating, *The Heart of the Diaconate*

We have already observed that the Servant Mysteries reveal truths that can't be discovered apart from Divine Revelation. Indeed, because they make known Christ the Servant in ways that human effort alone cannot, these mysteries share many of the traits associated with Divine Revelation. One trait is the distinction between what the theological tradition calls the objective and subjective dimensions of faith. Applied to the Servant Mysteries, this distinction gives rise to an essential insight that allows the deacon to internalize these mysteries. As such, they become *his* mysteries, *his* insights, revealing Christ the Servant in an ever-deepening way, calling him to an even more profound communion.

The objective and subjective dimensions of the Faith are expressed in the distinction between the *fides quae* and the *fides qua*. The *fides quae* is the objective dimension of the Faith and concerns what the Church holds in terms of her body of beliefs. In its most basic sense, it's that which is to be believed by the believer. Complementing the *fides quae* is the *fides qua*. This is the subjective dimension of the Faith and concerns the believer's belief. It's essentially the believer's own personal faith. Properly understood, the objective content of the Faith ought to form and inform our subjective adherence to the Faith. Simply put, the Faith of the Church shapes and transforms our personal faith.

The *fides quae* and *fides qua* describe a necessary relationship between what is objectively revealed to the believer in an extrinsic sense and what that same believer subjectively appropriates in an intrinsic sense. Both the objective and subjective dimensions must be held in tension in order for each to express its true meaning. In other words, in order for our faith to be authentic and its goal of salvation to be realized, we must not simply grasp on an intellectual level what the Church believes (*fides quae*) but internalize that belief so that it becomes a personal lived faith (*fides qua*).

Applied to the Servant Mysteries, the objective dimension has external objects as its focus. These are things found outside of ourselves, things that we can know without bias in a dispassionate way. This would include the ways in which Christ the Servant is revealed in such sources as Scripture, Tradition, the Magisterium, the lives of the saints, the sacraments, and even ministry. The subjective dimension of the Servant Mysteries has as its focus our interiority, realized in our will, intellect, memories, emotions, and desires. For the Servant Mysteries to become *my servant mysteries*, for them to be internalized and have a transformative effect, both the objective and the subjective dimensions must be held in tension. This tension is essential in order for each dimension to express its true meaning. In other words, in order for these mysteries to reveal Christ the Servant, and for this revelation to be incarnated in my life and ministry, I must not simply grasp on an intellectual level what these mysteries reveal (*fides quae*) but also internalize that revelation so that it becomes my personal revelation (*fides qua*).

For some, the term "subjective" has come to imply an overly emotive, somewhat arbitrary, and even capricious knowledge. This happens when the subjective dimension is untethered from the objective dimension, such that the deacon becomes relativistic. This form of relativism isolates him from his order. He becomes the source of his own diaconate, often making it up as he goes along. As a result, instead of incarnating Christ the Servant, he incarnates himself and, with himself, his faults and failures. This is why the objective dimension is essential to the subjective dimension: It provides a necessary corrective against a purely subjective approach to the deacon's vocation. Likewise, the subjective dimension provides a necessary corrective against a purely objective approach to this same vocation. Rather than inducing a balance where we continually teeter back and forth, this positive tension brings integration.

This integration enables the deacon to become more fully who he is. Such a self-realization is only possible when the interior life holds a primary place. The deacon really can't know Christ the Servant on a deeply personal level unless that knowledge moves from the exterior to the interior. He really can't have intimate communion with Christ unless he allows the objective dimension of the Servant Mysteries to move into his subjectivity, to infuse through grace every aspect of his being.

This movement from the objective to the subjective isn't static but rather admits of a kind of reciprocal dynamic. The more the deacon encounters the Servant Mysteries on the outside, the more he wants to appropriate Christ the Servant on the inside. Conversely, the more he appropriates Christ the Servant on the inside, the more he wants to encounter Him on the outside. In this dynamic, divine love is so palpable, so real, that the deacon desires to abandon himself to the Divine Presence revealed to him. His life and priorities are ordered more and more to Christ the Servant. Christ becomes more real to him in the sacrament of the present moment because the encounter is no longer simply external but internal. Because the deacon has internalized Christ the Servant, He now comes with the deacon throughout his day and continues His salvific mission through him. The deacon recognizes Christ the Servant in others on the outside because he knows Him intimately on the inside.

APPLYING THE SACRAMENT OF THE PRESENT MOMENT

> *To be satisfied with the present moment is to delight*
> *in it, and to adore the divine will in all that has to*
> *be done or suffered in all that succession of events*
> *that fill, as they pass, each present moment.*
> **Jean-Pierre de Caussade,**
> ***Abandonment to Divine Providence***

As noted earlier, the Servant Mysteries are the revelation of Christ the Servant as made known in the sacrament of the present moment. These mysteries enable the deacon to grow in his diaconate, bearing witness to Christ the Servant in preeminent and exemplary ways. With this in mind, and having explored such themes as woundedness, along with the need to internalize the Servant Mysteries, we now turn to examine how these mysteries are to permeate and penetrate the entire life of the deacon. We will do this by once again applying de Caussade's sacrament of the present moment. Recall that the sacrament of the present moment is the realization that the ever-present God makes himself known to us through everyday events such as the people we meet, the places we go, and even our struggles. It represents, as we've seen, a kind of personal revelation that is constant and ongoing. Unlike other kinds of personal revelation, it doesn't concern itself with something specific such as a vocation, job, or house but instead focuses on an ongoing awareness of God's presence in the here and now.

Because the deacon was configured to Christ the Servant at his ordination, it is Christ who calls the deacon to himself in and through the Servant Mysteries. In this respect, the Servant Mysteries don't simply reveal Christ the Servant; they make Him sacramentally present and, through Him, provide access to the inner life of the Trinity. Abandonment to divine providence, as applied to the diaconate, means abandonment to Christ the Servant, a life that lives out the Servant Mysteries rather than merely praying or meditating on them. The deacon becomes, through a participation in the sanctifying grace proper to his ordination, a servant mystery himself, revealing in his words and actions the Servant Mystery that is Christ Jesus.

By cultivating an interior life grounded in the Servant Mysteries, the deacon is drawn into a deep, interpersonal communion with Christ the Servant. Here, he is filled with a love that's not his own, given a vision that's not his own, and provided a strength that's not his own. Yet at the same time, that love, that vision, and that strength so imbue his life, so wound him to his core, that they become his in a certain sense. This means that the Servant Mysteries are realized in the sacrament of the present moment regardless of where the deacon is in that moment, whether it's the interior or exterior life, whether it's at prayer or in ministry, whether it's with his wife or with his children.

This approach means not only bringing Christ the Servant to those we meet, but seeing Christ the Servant in those very same people. It might be asked, "How can this be? How can we be Christ and at the same time see Him?" While it's certainly true that Christ isn't present to us as He was when He walked the earth some 2,000 years ago, He is nonetheless sacramentally present in at least three ways. First, insofar as we are all created in the image of God and insofar as Jesus is God, the image of Christ is present in everyone. Indeed, because the deacon by virtue of his calling is attuned to the Servant Mysteries, he sees by default Christ the Servant in all those he encounters. In Saint Matthew's "Judgment of the Nations," Jesus speaks directly of this with respect to service:

> Then the king will say to those on his right, "Come, you who are blessed by my Father. Inherit the kingdom prepared for you from the foundation of the world. For I was hungry and you gave me food, I was thirsty and you gave me drink, a stranger and you welcomed me, naked and you clothed me, ill and you cared for me, in prison and you visited me." Then the righteous will answer him and say, "Lord, when did we see you hungry and feed you, or thirsty and give you drink? When did we see you a stranger and welcome you, or naked and clothe you? When did we see you ill or in prison, and visit you?" And the king will say to them in reply, "Amen, I say to you, whatever you did for one of these least brothers of mine, you did for me." (Mt 25:34–40)

Second, we often see things in their absence, juxtaposing that which is there with that which is lacking. Regarding those we serve, our sensitivity to Christ the Servant helps us move beyond the superficial to a deeper reality. We know, because of the intimacy we share with Christ the Servant, that suffering doesn't indicate the absence of God, but instead His presence. In this paradox, we encounter the love of God precisely in and through

His suffering, such that suffering reveals Him and His great love for us in a way that nothing else does. He is the Suffering Servant, present in those who suffer.

This paradox is poignantly illustrated by the Romanian-born American writer Elie Wiesel in his moving book *Night*. At the height of the Holocaust, a young Elie and his father were imprisoned in a Nazi concentration camp. Elie recalls at one point being forced to watch the hanging of a boy. The boy weighed so little that the noose failed to break his neck, agonizingly prolonging his death. Others were then forced to weigh him down by hanging on his feet. In the midst of this, Elie heard someone ask, "For God's sake, where is God?" He then heard a voice within himself respond, saying, "Where is He? This is where — hanging here from this gallows."[21]

Finally, we see Christ the Servant reflected in the eyes of those we serve. Just as it's impossible to touch without simultaneously being touched, so too it's impossible to bring Christ the Servant without seeing a reflection of ourselves acting in the person of that same Christ. Of course, this realization requires a modicum of interior attentiveness; it is particularly obvious when, after the completion of an aspect of our ministry in which we have satisfied some need, we experience an internal satisfaction. This satisfaction arises because we have fulfilled the will of the One who sent us, completing our mission as emissaries. Figuratively speaking, we see in the eyes of those we serve a reflection of the love of a good and faithful servant: We see ourselves acting as Christ the Servant. Not only does this reflection reveal what we are — deacons — but more importantly, it affirms and strengthens our identity. It helps us to know we are doing the will of the One who sent us and, in a certain sense, incarnating Him by extending His hands from heaven to earth. This is how the deacon fulfills his role in the mystery of salvation. He be-

---

[21] Elie Wiesel, *Night* (New York: Bantam Books, 1982), 61.

comes more fully what he is.

Because the Servant Mysteries sacramentally reveal Christ the Servant and because abandonment to divine providence is experienced in the sacrament of the present moment, the Servant Mysteries are revealed in every moment, in ways big and small, profound and subtle. If the deacon is attentive to his diaconate, if he cultivates the Servant Mysteries in his interior life, his whole vision is transformed, and with it his entire life. He encounters these mysteries in his ministry, in his marriage, and in his fatherhood. He observes them in his prayers, meditations, and devotions. He perceives them in the workplace, while shopping, and with his friends. He recognizes them in the celebration of the sacraments, in *lectio,* and in reading pious literature.

Perhaps most powerfully, the deacon encounters the Servant Mysteries in the Holy Sacrifice of the Mass, through the penitential act, the Gloria, and the collects. He hears them in the Liturgy of the Word, the proclamation of the Gospel, the homily, the Creed, and the universal prayers. He experiences them more intensely in the Eucharistic prayers and, in particular, in the reception of Holy Communion. There he encounters, in the most sublime and inspiring way, the Servant Mystery himself, present — Body, Blood, Soul, and Divinity — in the Eucharistic species. Holy Communion becomes for the deacon a unique encounter with the One who sends him, Christ the Servant. Finally, he recognizes the Servant Mysteries in the very dismissal he gives to the people, which requires that he take what he has received on a personal level, Christ the Servant, and bring Him to the world. In all of this, the Servant Mysteries aren't one aspect of the deacon's life; rather, they are to permeate and penetrate every aspect of it. The deacon is to live and breathe these mysteries and, in doing so, to continue to fulfill the will of the One who sends him.

Chapter Four
Living the Servant Mysteries

To fulfill his mission, the deacon therefore needs a deep interior life, sustained by the exercises of piety recommended by the Church. Carrying out ministerial and apostolic activities, fulfilling possible family and social responsibilities and, lastly, practicing an intense personal life of prayer require of the deacon, whether celibate or married, that unity of life which can only be attained, as Vatican Council II taught, through deep union with Christ.

Pope Saint John Paul II, Address to the Plenary Assembly of the Congregation for the Clergy, November 30, 1995

Some years back, I had the opportunity to make a retreat under the direction of Deacon James Keating. The retreat involved only one retreatant other than myself. It was held in Omaha during one of the summer sessions of the Institute of Priestly Formation (IPF), where Keating was the director of theological formation. The retreat's central tenet, built around the principles of relationship, identity, and mission (known by the acronym RIM), was developed by IPF's executive director, Father Richard Gabuzda, and first delivered in a paper for one of their symposiums.[1]

As Keating explained RIM and applied it to the diaconate, I was immediately captivated by its elegant simplicity. It put into words something that had been stirring in my heart for many years. Similar to the experience of many in priestly formation, much of my diaconal formation has lacked a solid spiritual dimension. Sure, all formation programs address spirituality, but quite often they do so in a rather external, dispassionate, and objective sense, leaving it up to the candidate to make of it what he will. This seems to me grossly lacking. This deficiency has been compounded by how little the Church has understood her own diaconate since the order was restored by the Second Vatican Council. Unlike the priesthood, which has developed over the centuries a robust theology upon which to build a spirituality, the diaconate has had but a rudimentary and fragmented theology. Since all spiritualities, by their very natures, are grounded in the sources of Revelation and expressed in Tradition, this lack of a clear theology has complicated matters. Without a clear sense of what the diaconate is and what its place within the mystery of salvation is, it's difficult to develop an authentic diaconal spirituality.

The central mission of the IPF is to place spiritual formation

---

[1] Richard Gabuzda, "Relationship, Identity, Mission: A Proposal for Spiritual Formation," in *2005 Symposium, Interiority for Mission: Spiritual Formation for Priests of the New Evangelization*, ed. Edward Mathews (Omaha: IPF Publications, 2005), 39–51.

at the heart of priestly formation. Using three easy-to-grasp, interrelated terms — relationship, identity, and mission — Gabuzda was able to articulate a dynamic that describes priestly spirituality. At the retreat, Keating applied this same dynamic, with modifications, to the diaconate. I was stunned and immediately began to sketch out how this application would look graphically, considering the implications not simply for diaconal spirituality but for the entire life and ministry of the deacon.

Before describing RIM and its application to the diaconate, I want to look further into an observation just made — namely, that without a clear sense of what the diaconate is, and its place within the mystery of salvation, it's difficult to develop an authentic diaconal spirituality. Such a novel approach to the theology and spirituality of the diaconate requires a new look at the origins of the diaconate and how the diaconate relates to the presbyterate and the episcopate. It requires a look that reaches back beyond the call of the Seven (see Acts 6:1–6), grounding the order as an integral part of God's plan of salvation.

REVEALING THE ORIGINS OF THE DIACONATE

Ephrem, honored by Christian tradition with the title "Harp of the Holy Spirit," remained a deacon of the Church throughout his life. It was a crucial and emblematic decision: he was a deacon, a servant, in his liturgical ministry, and more radically, in his love for Christ, whose praises he sang in an unparalleled way, and also in his love for his brethren, whom he introduced with rare skill to the knowledge of divine Revelation.
Pope Benedict XVI, General Audience, November 28, 2007

Some years ago, I quite providentially stumbled upon the unity of Holy Orders while exploring the origins of the diaconate in my book *In the Person of Christ the Servant*. Applying the personalist thought and language of Pope Saint John Paul II to diaconal ministry, I defined the diaconate as not so much something we do, but rather someone we give, our very selves. This gift-of-self, which is simply another way of speaking about love, intrigued me, especially as it played out in the Paschal Mystery. It was there that I discovered what I would later call the Establishment Hypothesis.

The Establishment Hypothesis is grounded in three fundamental principles. First, and most importantly, the Paschal Mystery — that is to say, Christ's Passion, Death, and Resurrection — is the source of our salvation (see CCC 571). Second, God offers this salvation through His Church, by way of the Sacrament of Holy Orders (CCC 1536). Third, just as the Paschal Mystery was nothing less than a divine gift-of-self, so too it is perpetuated through a similar gift-of-self in the three degrees of Holy Orders. Bishops, priests, and deacons, as good disciples, follow Christ's example by their own gifts-of-self, their own acts of love.

In many respects, the Last Supper isn't only part of the Paschal Mystery; it encapsulates it. The Church has long looked to this event as the institution of the priesthood along with the episcopacy, which is the fullness of Holy Orders. If there is a cohesive unity to be found in Holy Orders, then it would make sense that it should be found in the Paschal Mystery; and because this mystery is encapsulated in the Last Supper, the Last Supper should be our starting point.

On the night before He died, Jesus shared the Passover meal with the Twelve. During the meal, He issued two distinct sets of commands. The first set is found in the Synoptic Gospels: "Take and eat … Take and drink … Do this in memory of me …" (see Mt 26:17–30; Mk 14:12–26; Lk 22:7–39). These are known as the "institutional narratives," as they simultaneously institute the Eucharist and the priesthood. However, during that same meal Jesus issued another set of commands; this is found not in the Synoptics but in John's Gospel. In John, after washing the feet of His disciples, Jesus says, "I have given you a model to follow, so that as I have done for you, you should also do" (Jn 13:15). This command is known as the *mandatum*. On Holy Thursday, the *Ceremonial of Bishops* calls for the bishop to begin the foot washing by removing his chasuble, under which is his dalmatic. Pope Francis, during the same ritual, refashions his priestly stole into a diaconal stole before washing the feet of the people. They wear the garb of deacons because although they are bishops, they still possess the diaconate, and there is something intuitively diaconal about the act of washing feet.

In the Last Supper, this one event that encapsulates the whole of the Paschal Mystery, we have two sets of dominical commands: one unmistakably priestly in nature and the other unmistakably diaconal. In this respect, the Establishment Hypothesis isn't really new. Deacon James Keating writes: "The foot washing scene at the Last Supper is an expression of the institution of the diaconate by Christ, since it reflects the doctrinal truth of the unity of Holy Orders. There is symmetry between Christ's charge to the Apostles: '*Do this* in memory of me' (Luke 22:19) and his other apostolic charge '*You should also do* as I have done to you' (John 13:14–15)."[2] In making this claim, Keating cites Cardinal Walter Kasper, who in a paper asserts:

> We have seen that without *diaconia* there cannot be a Church, because Christ himself is one who serves (Luke 22:27). Therefore, at the Last Supper … he not only established the idea of priesthood, but, in principle, also *laid the foundation of the diaconal ministry*. By the wash-

---

[2] Keating, *Heart of the Diaconate*, 64.

ing of feet, he gave us an example, so that we also do, as he did to us (John 13:15). In these words, one can see the foundation of the diaconate.[3]

Where the Establishment Hypothesis breaks new ground, and where it moves beyond Keating's and Kasper's intuitive observations, is that it describes precisely how this happens through a series of successive gifts-of-self (acts of love). Critical to the hypothesis is the fundamental reality that we simply can't give what we don't first possess. In other words, if the apostles didn't receive the fullness of what we now call "Holy Orders" from Christ, they couldn't pass it on to the bishops. Likewise, if the bishops didn't receive Holy Orders from the apostles, they couldn't pass it on to priests and deacons. In a similar fashion, if priests and deacons didn't receive their orders from the bishops, they couldn't pass it on to the laity in the form of priestly and diaconal ministry. This progression is grounded in the principle *nemo dat quod non habet*, literally meaning "no one gives what they don't have."

To better appreciate this progression as it relates the diaconate to the mystery of salvation, I'll break the Establishment Hypothesis down into seven simple steps that refer to the diagram in Figure 1. In considering these steps and the diagram that illustrates them, it's important to notice how the steps are distinguished by discrete gifts-of-self that form an organic continuity of sorts. Each step, and the group it represents, follows the preceding step and group as a kind of emissary or envoy. Equally important to notice is how the Establishment Hypothesis reveals that the entire Church is meant to be a servant Church and that the diaconate stands as a model and exemplar after Christ the Servant. The steps are as follows:

---

[3] Walter Kasper, "The Deacon Offers an Ecclesiological View of the Present-Day Challenges in the Church and Society" (Paper given at IDC Study-Conference, Brixen, Italy, October 1997).

Step 1: Through His Gift-of-Self on the Cross, Jesus reconciles humanity to the Father; this offer of reconciliation is encapsulated and memorialized in the Last Supper.

Step 2: In the Last Supper, Jesus issues two sets of commands to His apostles, one priestly (Eucharist) and the other diaconal (*mandatum*).

Step 3: These commands, in light of the Paschal Mystery, establish both the priesthood and the diaconate.

Step 4: The apostles, having received this Gift-of-Self from Christ in the form of the priesthood and diaconate, now gift themselves, in the form of that same priesthood and diaconate, to their successors, the bishops (see *Lumen Gentium*, 20).

Step 5: The bishops, having received this gift-of-self from the apostles in the form of the priesthood and diaconate, now gift themselves to priests and deacons through the conferral of Holy Orders.

Step 6: The priests and deacons, having received this gift-of-self from the bishops in the form of the priesthood and diaconate, now reveal in a distinctive and complementary manner the whole Christ (*Christus totus*). As a result, they gift themselves to the laity through evangelizing and the sacraments.

Step 7: The laity, having received this gift-of-self from priests and deacons, now gift themselves in the living out of their vocations for the salvation of the world.

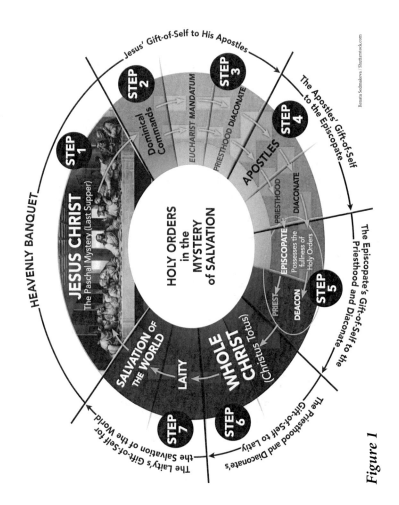

Renata Sedmakova / Shutterstock.com

Figure 1

RECONCILING ACTS 6 WITH THE ESTABLISHMENT HYPOTHESIS

"Brothers, select from among you seven reputable men,
filled with the Spirit and wisdom, whom we shall appoint
to this task, whereas we shall devote ourselves to prayer
and to the ministry of the word." The proposal was
acceptable to the whole community, so they chose Stephen,
a man filled with faith and the holy Spirit, also Philip,
Prochorus, Nicanor, Timon, Parmenas, and Nicholas of
Antioch, a convert to Judaism. They presented these men
to the apostles who prayed and laid hands on them.
Acts 6:3–6

Given the unanimous witness of the Tradition, the question arises of how we can reconcile the institution of the Seven (see Acts
6:1–6) with the Establishment Hypothesis. One way to address
this apparent conflict is through the distinction between *officium*
(office) and *ordo* (order). Whereas an office is a position in a larg-
er organization that carries with it a specific function, an order
is an office shared by two or more forming a recognized body.
In the sequence of causality, an office always precedes an order.
Before a man can enter the order of bishops, there must first be
an episcopal office. Similarly, before a man can enter the order of
presbyters, there must first be a presbyteral office. Likewise, before someone can enter the order of deacons, there must first be a
diaconal office.

While the *mandatum* established the office of deacon, the se-
lection of the Seven and the laying on of hands represent the institution of the diaconal order. While the office represents a kind of
conception, the order represents a kind of birth.

There is some implicit evidence for this progression in the
Scriptures. We know, for example, that the presbyteral office was

established at the Last Supper. However, the presbyteral order was instituted sometime after, as witnessed by Luke (see Acts 15:6, 23) and Peter (1 Pt 5:1). Likewise, we can say that the episcopal office (the fullness of orders) was also established at the Last Supper. However, the episcopal order was instituted sometime after, as witnessed by Timothy (1 Tm 3). If this is true of the presbyterate and episcopate, then it's reasonable to conclude that it's also true of the diaconate.

Christ's total Gift-of-Self means that the complementary relationship among the episcopacy, priesthood, and diaconate finds its nexus in the one person of Christ. Each order participates and contributes in a unique way toward bringing the *Christus totus* ("the whole Christ") to the world. Using Pope Saint John Paul II's personalist language, we discover not only a new way of envisioning the origins of the diaconate but, perhaps even more important, an organic way of speaking about the unity of Holy Orders.

If the above is true, and I believe it is, then the diaconate isn't ancillary to God's plan of salvation; it is an absolutely integral and indispensable component born in the mind of the Father before all ages. We now possess a firm basis by which we can develop a diaconal spirituality based on RIM and distinguish it clearly from priestly spirituality.

RELATIONSHIP, IDENTITY, AND MISSION

> *We should always look to God as in ourselves, no*
> *matter in what manner we meditate upon Him,*
> *so as to accustom ourselves to dwell in His Divine*
> *Presence. For when we behold Him within our souls,*
> *all our powers and faculties, and even our senses, are*
> *recollected within us. If we look at God apart from*
> *ourselves, we are easily distracted by exterior objects.*
> **Saint Margaret Mary Alacoque,** *Letters*

In our consideration of RIM, it won't be necessary to go into great detail, as the fundamental building blocks of this dynamic have already been laid in the first three chapters. We need only pull it all together and make the necessary connections. Recall that we began with the primacy of the interior life, which requires an abandonment to Christ the Servant in and through the Servant Mysteries. This is the emphasis that gives diaconal spirituality its definitive character, and it's this same emphasis that provides a starting point for the application of RIM to the diaconate.

The three elements of RIM provide a way of describing diaconal spirituality and, equally importantly, form the necessary bridge between the deacon's interior and exterior lives. It's a simple concept that allows us to move what we've discussed so far from the theoretical to the practical. Figure 2 illustrates the association between these three elements, and the following description explains how they correspond to de Caussade's *Abandonment to Divine Providence*.

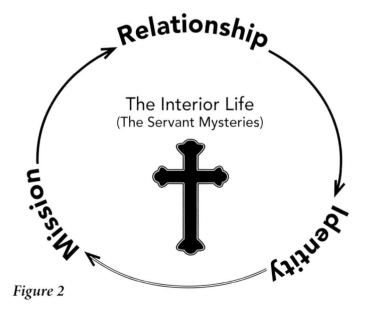

Figure 2

Relationship: The inner part of the circle represents the interior life, where, in response to being configured to Christ the Servant at ordination, we prayerfully contemplate the Servant Mysteries. This is the "place" of ongoing encounter with the One who calls us to himself. This call, properly understood as our vocation, isn't so much a call to something (the diaconate), but a call to Someone (Christ Jesus) in and through that something (the diaconate). It's an invitation to share in the inner life of the Trinity by way of our vocation and, in doing so, bear witness to Christ the Servant. Here, our witness rises and falls in direct proportion to the intimacy we share with Christ. It's precisely within this call and our response that a new relationship — begun at our creation, consecrated at our Baptism, strengthened in Confirmation, purified in Reconciliation, and nourished in the Eucharist — takes root. As a result of ordination, we now relate to Christ and His Church in a new way, in a diaconal way. This, of course, requires full, active, and conscious participation with the sanctifying grace that accompanies Holy Orders. Our interior configuration at ordination and our response to it through ongoing meditation on the Servant Mysteries foster a particular kind of relationship. This relationship enables us to come to know and love, in a deep and abiding way, the One who calls us, making possible our diaconal witness to the world.

Relationship corresponds to de Caussade's notion of abandonment, though the terms are not quite synonymous. Abandonment bespeaks the quality of the relationship in which one or both parties surrender their will to the other. It's an act of love, expressed in a gift-of-self, implying full confidence that what is surrendered, while vulnerable, remains safe. Though abandonment is typically spoken of as a surrender of the will, the will, as a power of the soul, really signifies the entire person. It's the seat of his choices, which are the result of a deliberation of the intellect. Indeed, it's through the will that the person manifests his very self to the world in and through specific concrete acts. The will moves the interior life to the exterior and back again. As such, to abandon the will is to surrender one's self willingly to another. As we've already observed, such an abandonment isn't a relinquishing of responsibility, a kind of spiritual cop-out, but instead a willingness to unite our will with Christ the Servant in the complete confidence that through this union, and only through this union, our lives will be fulfilled.

Abandonment, as we've already seen, isn't a single event. Rather, it's a lifelong series of events that enable the deacon to share his life with Christ Jesus. It's precisely within this close sharing that intimacy is experienced and deepened. These events are begun in the interior life as that interior life encounters the Servant Mysteries in the sacrament of the present moment. This could be in prayer or meditation, in ministry or at work, in being a husband or father — in fact, in any endeavor of life. While these present moments arise in the exterior life, they reveal the Servant Mysteries when they are consciously brought into the interior life. These mysteries don't simply make Christ the Servant present to the deacon; rather, they reveal in a profound way Christ's unique and unconditional love for him. It's this ongoing revelation that invites the deacon to greater abandonment and, with it, greater intimacy.

Identity: Within this relationship of abandonment, we experience the beauty that is God and are wounded at the depths of our soul. This woundedness, as we've already seen, brings about a transformation such that we gain a new identity, much as courtship brings about a change in identity for the man and woman. At some point in time, the two are so struck with each other that they marry and their relationship reaches such an intensity that he is now *husband* and she is now *wife*. While they remain the same people, they now see and understand who they are in a fundamentally different way. The same is true with the diaconate. At some point in the discernment process, the man's intimacy with Christ matures, requiring by a positive act of the will a choice that will forever change him. As in marriage, this change reveals a fundamental truth — that relationship gives rise to identity. Our connectedness to another shapes who we are. Thus, a husband is only a husband in relation to his wife, and a deacon is only a deacon in relation to Christ the Servant. The more intense the relationship, the greater its impact on identity. As a result, as the relationship grows or diminishes, identity grows or diminishes in direct proportion.

The analogy between marriage and the diaconate as it pertains to identity can only go so far. Whereas in marriage the union is sacramental and dissolves at death, in ordination the relationship is ontological in nature. This means that it imparts an indelible character to the soul. While a married man can cease to be married, as when his wife dies, a deacon can never cease to be a deacon. This identity has been infused in his "spiritual DNA," and even if he should deny his faith and burn in the fires of hell, he will do so as a deacon. Thus, relationship gives rise to identity. We know who we are based on our connectedness to and intimacy with another.

It's important to recognize that this new identity isn't something other than who we are. We don't become someone else, adopting foreign traits and strange ways. Rather, if the relationship is healthy, this new identity strengthens and fulfills who we already know ourselves to be. In many respects, we become more fully who we are, more fully alive. This is simply an application of grace perfecting nature. We receive the sanctifying grace at ordination through an intense encounter that configures us to Christ the Servant. This grace capacitates us to rise above the effects of sin, enabling us to become what God fully intends us to be, revealing who we really are. Saint Thomas Aquinas asserts,

"Although man is inclined to an end by nature, yet he cannot attain that end by nature, but only by grace because of the exalted character of the end."[4] Applied here, the specific sanctifying grace associated with the diaconate enables the deacon to be deacon and, through that identity, realize his final end: intimate communion with the Trinity forever. The grace of the diaconate gives us a sense of who we really are. In this respect, we so identify with Christ the Servant that in a certain sense, we become Christ the Servant by incarnating Him in our lives.

Mission: Pope Saint John Paul II was fond of remarking that the Church doesn't have a mission, she *is* a mission. In his 1990 encyclical *Redemptoris Missio*, he writes, "This definitive self-revelation of God is the fundamental reason why the Church is missionary by her very nature. She cannot do other than proclaim the Gospel."[5] Understood this way, mission stands at the very heart of the Church; it's her reason for being, her sole focus, and thus her highest work. This work, though singular in purpose, admits of a diversity of expression. Returning to the thought of John Paul II: "Mission is a single but complex reality, and it develops in a variety of ways."[6] While all of the faithful belong to this mission and the discipleship it entails, the clergy are called to live out this mission in a specific way. As the *Catechism* observes:

> Holy Orders is the sacrament through which the mission entrusted by Christ to his apostles continues to be exercised in the Church until the end of time: thus it is the sacrament of apostolic ministry. It includes three degrees: episcopate, presbyterate, and diaconate. (1536)

---

[4] Thomas Aquinas, *Super Boethius de Trinitate,* q.6, a.4, ad 5, cited in Brian Mullady, *Man's Desire for God* (Bloomington, IN: 1stBooks, 2003), 19.

[5] *Redemptoris Missio*, 5.

[6] Ibid., 41.

The mission of the diaconate, like that of all the faithful, always takes place within the broader context of the mission Christ entrusted to His Church. It's a specific participation in and realization of the call to go and make disciples of all nations (see Mt 28:19). Each of the three degrees of Holy Orders shares in the Church's mission in a way that corresponds to its particular role in the life of the Church. Hence, we can speak of a diaconal participation that has as its defining character a preeminent witness to Christ the Servant. The mission of the diaconate is inextricably tied to the mission of the Church, which itself is inextricably bound to Christ's mission of salvation. The deacon's mission is realized not only in the many ministries that flow from his diaconate, but most importantly, in the witness of his life. Of this, Pope Saint John Paul II writes, "Without witnesses there can be no witness, just as without missionaries there can be no missionary activity."[7] The deacon's way of life is one that shines out to others and beckons them to a more excellent way (see 1 Cor 12:31ff).

The deacon's call to bear witness in his life and ministry is grounded in his identity and sourced in his relationship with Christ the Servant. Where, as we've seen earlier, relationship gives rise to identity, identity now gives rise to mission. We know what to do (mission) based on who we are (identity). The moment a man becomes a husband, he has a whole new set of responsibilities. Likewise, the moment a man becomes a deacon, he has a whole new ministry. Based on the Latin maxim *agere sequitur esse* ("action follows being"), mission flows from identity.

Identity gives mission a personal quality that differentiates it among missionaries. So, for example, two women are sitting in a room, one a mother, the other a babysitter. The mother's child is playing nearby and falls. Both women react, but in very differ-

---

[7] Ibid., 61.

ent ways. Though the babysitter cares for the child, she isn't the mother. It's the mother who instinctively jumps up and quickly attends the child. Her relationship with the child gives rise to the mother's identity, and it's this very identity that leads her to exercise her mission in a way different from the babysitter. This in no way diminishes the care given by the babysitter. Her identity as a babysitter gives her a different relationship with the child; because of the nature of this relationship, she can quit at any time, which is not so for the mother.

This analogy is also helpful in distinguishing the mission of a deacon from that of a lay minister. Both may be able to do the same thing equally well, such as proclaim the Gospel, but not in quite the same way. This is because identity matters. The deacon's identity is grounded in his relationship to Christ the Servant as a result of his ordination. Consequently, his mission will admit of a different quality than the layperson's, much the same way as the priest's mission will differ from the deacon's. To the extent that diaconal identity grows or diminishes, diaconal ministry and its unique contribution to the mission of the Church grow or diminish in proportion.

Mission corresponds to de Caussade's notion of duty, in which duty is understood as revealing God's will in a particular moment. If, in the present moment, we perceive the suffering Christ in others, then our duty arising from that perception is an act of love, and that act of love is nothing less than the exercise of our diaconal mission. Without the sacrament of the present moment, without recognizing Christ throughout our day, we can pass right by Him. He will go hidden in our hearts, concealed in our ministry, and ultimately unnoticed in our lives. The sacrament of the present moment reveals that the Servant Mysteries are everywhere. They permeate and penetrate all aspects of reality precisely because Christ the Servant does the same. He is constantly revealing the divine will. Of this de Caussade observes:

There is not a moment in which God does not present himself under the cover of some pain to be endured, of some consolation to be enjoyed, or of some duty to be performed. All that takes place within us, around us, or through us, contains and conceals His divine action.[8]

PUTTING IT ALL TOGETHER

Mission, as an act of divine love expressed in diaconal ministry, completes the RIM circle and at the very same time begins it anew. This is because, in the very carrying out of his mission, the deacon grows in intimate communion with Christ the Servant. This enriches his relationship, which in turn deepens his identity, rendering his mission even more effective. The same is true in marriage. When a couple engage in their mission of a shared life, resolving conflicts, raising children, and so forth, they grow in intimacy. That increased intimacy enhances the relationship, which in turn deepens their identities as husband and wife, rendering their mission even more effective. Thus, far from being a static once-around-the-circle reality, RIM is a dynamic that can continue throughout the life of the deacon. Integrating the interior and exterior aspects of his life enables him to continually discover the Servant Mysteries in the sacrament of the present moment. This integration capacitates him, through grace, to incarnate these mysteries revealing Christ the Servant and in the process to fulfill his mission.

Beyond its simple elegance, RIM is universal. We've already seen its application to the diaconate and to marriage. We know it's being employed with seminarians at the Institute of Priestly Formation. This is but a small sampling of its wide relevance in the life of the Church. Imagine a deacon assigned to promote evangelization in his parish. Instead of doing what's typically done by selecting an off-the-shelf program, gathering his team,

---

[8] De Caussade, *Abandonment*, 16.

and executing the effort, he begins by forming the formators with RIM. Long before he launches the ministry, he starts by focusing with his team on their relationship to Christ through a rediscovery — or, in many cases, a discovery — of the interior life. Through such pious practices as *lectio*, common prayer, retreats, and adoration, the team begins to deepen their relationship with Christ and with one another. Members bond, and a community forms. From this relationship, they develop a common identity, and only then, perhaps six months or a year later, do they engage in the mission of evangelization. The ministry benefits enormously from this earlier work because it is a fruit of cooperation with the Holy Spirit.

RIM provides a corrective to what I call the *rush to mission*. This rush arises out of a culture that places too much emphasis on functionality and too little on relationship, often reducing human beings to human doings. If, for instance, the pastor wants more extraordinary ministers of Holy Communion for Mass, we typically put an announcement in the bulletin, have a night or two of training in the functionality of dispensing Our Lord, and then assign ministers to various Masses. Little to no thought is given to the lay ministers' relationships or identities, often rendering their ministry void of the transformative power it possesses. Indeed, rather than serve to draw them to greater intimacy with the One who calls them to minister, this mode of formation can allow them to hide behind their ministry.

When ministry is reduced to the thing being done, ministers don't have to render themselves vulnerable and open up to Christ. All they have to do is punch their "piety ticket" by doing the ministry and then go home. As the psalmist says:

> For you do not desire sacrifice or I would give it;
>> a burnt offering you would not accept.
> My sacrifice, O God, is a contrite spirit;

> a contrite, humbled heart, O God, you will not
> scorn. (Ps 51:18–19)

Instead of giving God our very selves in ministry, we give him our work, emptied by the lack of relationship and identity. God does not desire our ministry. Rather, He desires *us* far more than we can ever desire Him. Ministry, then, as a participation in the mission of the Church, is the result of something more profound — relationship and identity. Without these two prior elements, mission is undermined and, with it, the very Gospel it attempts to proclaim.

While the relevancy of RIM in the spiritual and ministerial life of the deacon is quite apparent, its real power lies in its theological grounding. In this respect, we can easily correlate RIM's three elements to the Establishment Hypothesis, particularly as RIM pertains to Holy Orders (Figure 3). Here, our relationship, begun in creation, is deepened in intimacy through the Paschal Mystery as expressed in the Last Supper. Through the dominical command associated with the *mandatum*, this relationship gives rise to our identity as deacons. From this identity, we, along with bishops and priests, then make our contribution to the *Christus totus* to the laity, who make their own unique and indispensable contribution. In this way, we as deacons fulfill our mission within the much broader mission of the Church.

Figure 3

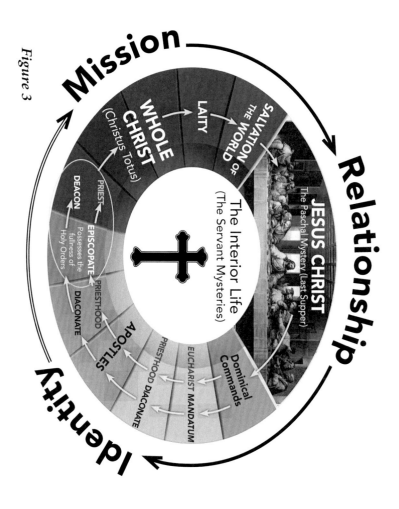

Mission

Relationship

Identity

WHOLE CHRIST
(Christus Totus)

LAITY

SALVATION OF THE WORLD

JESUS CHRIST
The Paschal Mystery (Last Supper)

The Interior Life
(The Servant Mysteries)

DEACON

PRIEST

EPISCOPATE
Possesses the fullness of Holy Orders

PRIESTHOOD
DIACONATE

APOSTLES

PRIESTHOOD DIACONATE

EUCHARIST MANDATUM

Dominical Commands

PRAYER OF ABANDONMENT AND LITTLE EXAMEN

> *If we neglect prayer and if the branch is not connected
> with the vine, it will die. That connecting of the branch
> to the vine is prayer. If that connection is there then love
> is there, then joy is there, and we will be the sunshine
> of God's love, the hope of eternal happiness, the flame
> of burning love. Why? Because we are one with Jesus.*
> **Saint Teresa of Calcutta,** *Everything Starts from Prayer*

The rich spiritual and mystical Tradition of the Church offers a treasure trove of devout practices, and divine abandonment represents only one of these. All require a certain level of discernment before they are undertaken. All involve considerable effort to maintain. All have similar pitfalls with regard to our steadfastness. No matter what we choose, it's really God who chooses us. Thus the grace necessary to persevere will be given — guaranteed (see 2 Cor 12:9)! That said, no practice is perfect this side of heaven. God doesn't call the perfect, only those willing to be perfected.

If you sense in prayer that God may be calling you to divine abandonment as described in this book, and if this is confirmed in conversation with your spiritual director, then you ought to begin a discernment process. There's no better way to discern a spiritual practice than by actually taking it up on a temporary basis.

Whether you decide to move forward with divine abandonment on a temporary or continual basis, the practice as laid out here is hardly burdensome. It presumes you're already praying the Divine Office and have other long-held devotions such as adoration, *lectio*, or the Rosary. It's meant to augment morning and evening prayer (or whatever your first and last prayer of the day happens to be) with a specialized Prayer of Abandonment and a Little Examen, respectively. These prayers are meant to catalyze our lives with a greater sensitivity to the Servant Mysteries as they are revealed in the sacrament of the present moment, be it in the interior or exterior dimensions of our lives.

The Prayer of Abandonment is drawn from the diaconal prayer of ordination and is said at the beginning of each day. As Jesus is the Primordial Servant Mystery and was manifest at our ordination, where He configured us to himself, the prayer harkens back to that moment, making it sacramentally present at the start of our day. It draws upon the supernatural, abundant storehouse of grace given to us when we received the gift of Christ the Servant.

Prayer of Abandonment

Almighty God, be present with me by your power. You are the source of all my honor, you assign me my rank, you give me my ministry.

So that I may grow in greater intimacy with you, and serve you in love and fidelity, I abandon my day, my hour, and indeed every moment of my life to you, Father, Son and Holy Spirit.

Free me from the snares of the Evil One and the attachments of this world, that I may always be what you want me to be, go where you want me to go, and do what you want me to do.

Help me to see you in the needs of those who suffer and to reach beyond my own limitations, making you present in the exercise of the gift of my diaconate. Make me ever conscious of the Servant Mysteries in the sacrament of the present moment so that I may excel in every virtue: in love that is sincere, in concern for the sick and the poor, in unassuming authority, in self-discipline, and in holiness in life.

May I remain strong and steadfast in Christ, giving to the world the witness of a pure conscience. May I in this life imitate your Son, who came not to be served but to serve, and one day reign with Him in heaven. I ask this through Christ our Lord. Amen.

Mary, Mother of the Diaconate, pray for me. *(Say three times.)*

Whereas the Prayer of Abandonment starts our day, the Little Examen ends it. The two are designed to work together, fixing our gaze firmly on Christ the Servant. The Little Examen isn't meant to replace a formal examination of conscience. If it's your practice to do a daily examination, I suggest you don't relinquish it but instead incorporate the Little Examen into it. I call this the Little Examen as, like the Prayer of Abandonment, it's meant not to supplant our current prayer routine but to supplement it. It's short and sweet, but in its brevity and simplicity it enables us to reflect back upon our day, acknowledging our successes and failures as they pertain to our abandonment. For the successes, for the times we became aware of the Servant Mysteries in the sacrament of the present moment, we give God thanks and praise, for it's only by responding to His grace that such an awareness is possible. Likewise, for the times when we've missed Him or even sought to avoid Him, we ask for His pardon and peace. The Prayer of Abandonment and the Little Examen work in conjunction with one another to help cultivate our interior life as deacons.

Little Examen

Almighty God, at the close of this day, I turn to you in

complete abandonment. I beg you, send your Holy Spirit upon me that I may now enter your peace, calling to mind my sins and shortcomings.

Brief period of silence.

Have I made a conscious effort today to perceive you in the sacrament of the present moment?

Where have I seen you, and how did I respond to your presence?

Where have I missed you?

Where have I deliberately ignored you?

For the times I was aware of your presence in the lives of those I encountered, I give you thanks and praise. For the times I failed to see you and for the times I failed to respond to your needs, I am truly sorry.

So that I may grow in greater intimacy with you and better bear witness to the world through the gift of my diaconate, I ask your pardon and peace.

Pray an Act of Contrition.

Mary, Mother of the Diaconate, pray for me. *(Say three times.)*

Conclusion

By responding to a divine call, the deacon enters into a new and more intimate relationship with Christ the Servant. In this relationship, he finds not only his identity but his mission as well. Inspired and informed by Christ's Gift-of-Self received at ordination, he is empowered by God to exercise his ministry in a way that actualizes his identity through sacred ecclesial service, the definitive characteristic of which is a salvific gift-of-self that wills the good of the other for the sake of the other. Thus each deacon finds within himself a summons that he cannot ignore, one that specifies his relationship to, his identity in, and his mission for Christ the Servant. As I noted at the conclusion of my book *In the Person of Christ the Servant,* it's a summons that can be expressed and realized in the phrase, "Deacons, become what you are."

If authentic renewal of the permanent diaconate is to take place — if deacons are to become more fully what they are —

it must begin with a rediscovery of the interior life rooted in a more comprehensive theology and realized in a more profound spirituality. Indeed, insofar as theology is in service to the spiritual life, this theology, when personally appropriated, can only serve to deepen the deacon's interior communion with Christ the Servant, further refining his identity and in the process rendering his ministry more effective. Together, the Establishment Hypothesis and RIM provide the theological basis and the spiritual structure to better integrate the interior and exterior lives of the deacon. They enable him, in the very exercise of his diaconate, to experience Christ the Servant and, in Him, a little heaven on earth.

Finally, this work would not be complete without being commended to the intercession of the Blessed Virgin Mary. Her example of humble service bore Christ the Servant into the world, giving the diaconate its perfect model. Beyond that, insofar as she is the mother of Christ the Servant and insofar as deacons are configured to that same Christ, she is our mother in the order of sacred service as well. With this in mind, to her many titles we can add one more: *Mater Diaconati* (Mother of the Diaconate). Joining our voice to hers, let us always respond to the call of the Holy Spirit by saying "We are the servants of the Lord. May it be done to us according to His word" (see Lk 1:38). *Sancta Maria, Mater Diaconati, ora pro nobis.*

Appendix
The Diaconal Prayer of Ordination

Almighty God, be present with us by your power. You are the source of all honor, you assign to each his rank, you give to each his ministry. You remain unchanged, but you watch over all creation and make it new through your Son, Jesus Christ, our Lord: He is your Word, your power, and your wisdom. You foresee all things in your eternal providence and make due provision for every age. You make the Church, Christ's Body, grow to its full stature as a new and greater temple. You enrich it with every kind of grace and perfect it with a diversity of members to serve the whole body in a wonderful pattern of unity. You established a threefold ministry of worship and service for the glory of your name. As ministers of your tabernacle you chose the sons of Levi and gave them your blessing as their everlasting inheritance. In the first days of your Church under the inspiration of the Holy Spirit the apostles of your Son appointed seven men of good repute to assist them in the daily ministry, so that they themselves might be more free for prayer and preaching. By prayer and the laying on of hands the apostles entrusted to those chosen men the ministry of serving at tables.

Lord, send forth upon them the Holy Spirit, that they may be strengthened by the gift of the sevenfold grace to carry out faithfully the work of the ministry. May they excel in every virtue: in love that is sincere, in concern for the sick and the poor, in unassuming authority, in self-discipline, and in holiness in life. May their conduct exemplify your commandments and lead your people to imitate their purity of life.

May they remain strong and steadfast in Christ, giving to the world the witness of a pure conscience. May they in this life imitate your Son, who came, not to be served but to serve, and one day reign with Him in heaven.[1]

---

[1] United States Conference of Catholic Bishops, *Rites of Ordination of a Bishop, of Priests, and of Deacons* (Washington, DC: USCCB, 2003).

About the Author

Deacon Dominic Cerrato, Ph.D., is editor of OSV's *The Deacon* magazine, executive director of Diaconal Ministries, and director of diaconal formation for the Diocese of Joliet. He also offers spiritual direction through the Pastoral Solutions Institute. Formerly, he served in full-time pastoral ministry, specializing in adult faith formation. He has taught theology at Franciscan University of Steubenville, Duquesne University of the Holy Ghost, and Holy Apostles College & Seminary. Ordained twenty-five years, Deacon Dominic is an author, a national speaker, and a retreat master. In 2020, he was appointed by Pope Francis to the international papal commission on women and the diaconate. He and his wife, Judith, have been married for thirty-eight years, and they have ten children and many grandchildren.

Serving deacons as they serve the Church

The Deacon is a bimonthly (6 issues/year) magazine that serves permanent deacons and deacon candidates as they serve the Church by helping them foster intimate communion with Christ the Servant.

Through a cultivation of the interior life, which leads to effective ministry, *The Deacon* contributes to the mission of the Church by making present the *totus Christus* (the "whole Christ") to the world. *The Deacon* seeks to build a community of men on fire for the diaconate through quality content that forms, informs and inspires.

Radiating joy, *The Deacon* is a trustworthy resource that accompanies deacons, deacon candidates and deacon directors as they live out, learn about and support diaconal ministry.

For more information or to start your subscription, visit **The-Deacon.com/subscribe**, or call **(800) 348-2440 and select option 2**.

Bulk and volume rates also available.